Why Men Stray
Why Men Stay

What Every Woman Needs to Know About Making the Commitment Last

SUSAN KELLEY

ADAMS MEDIA CORPORATION
Holbrook, Massachusetts

Published by Adams Media Corporation
260 Center Street, Holbrook, MA 02343

ISBN: 1-55850-634-9

Printed in the United States of America.

J   I   H   G   F   E   D   C   B

Library of Congress Cataloging-in-Publication Data
Kelley, Susan
Why men stray, why men stay : what every woman needs to know about making the commitment last / Susan Kelley.
p.   cm.
Includes index.
ISBN 1-55850-634-9 (pbk.)
1. Adultery—United States. 2. Married men—United States—Sexual behavior.
3. Married men—United States—Psychology. 4. Marriage—United States. I. Title.
HQ806.K45   1996
306.73'6—dc20   96–26130
CIP

This publication is designed to provide accurate and authoritative information with regard to the subject matter covered. It is sold with the understanding that the publisher is not engaged in rendering legal, accounting, or other professional advice. If legal advice or other expert assistance is required, the services of a competent professional person should be sought.
— From a *Declaration of Principles* jointly adopted by a Committee of the American Bar Association and a Committee of Publishers and Associations

The people and situations described in this book are real, but the names, places, personal histories, and identifying details of the situations have been changed. Any similarity between an individual or situation described in the book and a specific real person or event is purely coincidental.

This book is available at quantity discounts for bulk purchases.
For information, call 1-800-872-5627 (in Massachusetts, 617-767-8100).

Visit our home page at http://www.adamsmedia.com

For the men of significance in my life:

My father, Francis Connaughton,
and my five brothers, Ken, Brian, Gary, Blaine, and Michael
and especially
Timothy, the best son—witty and wise
and
William, my wonderful husband, who has shown me
by his actions the true meaning of
love, loyalty and commitment.

Table of Contents

ACKNOWLEDGMENTS

Special thanks to
Carol Gaskin, Timothy Curtin, and Jane Ward
And to the many contributors who generously shared their opinions
and personal experiences, including "The Ranchettes," all of whom
prefer to remain anonymous.

Introduction

Welcome, and congratulations! By choosing this book, you have shown that you want your marriage to work.

Why Men Stray, Why Men Stay unlocks the secrets of the male mind for women who want to know what makes one man faithful and another a straying Casanova. And what better way to find the real answers to that question than to go directly to the source and ask married men why they *stray* or *stay*? You'll see men as you've never seen them before. I *guarantee* that your eyes will be opened—and the information you learn may very well be the key to your long-term marital success.

As part of the research for this book, I asked hundreds of married men to share their stories. The ages of these men ranged from twenty-one to seventy-nine years. They'd been married from six months to fifty-five years, and came from a variety of occupations and backgrounds. The one thing they shared was a willingness to talk about their worries, desires, and behavior.

Experience has taught me that men will tell me just about everything without too much probing and prodding. Men seem much more likely to open their hearts and communicate with a woman than with another man on this subject. Their stories and their comments show men for whom they *really* are. You will learn how important it is to listen when men talk about their relationships, their frustrations, and their feelings about infidelity. You'll find that there are no hidden agendas—men are very much what they appear to be.

In fact, the idea for this book was inspired by a man. I was on a promotional tour for my previous book, *Why Men Commit.* He approached me after a TV show as I was leaving the stage. "Sure," he said, "you tell a woman how to get a man, but someone should tell her how to keep him from straying." His suggestion seemed like a perfect idea. *Why Men Stray, Why Men Stay* is a natural sequel to *Why Men Commit.* Commitment is only the first step in a long-term relationship, but to most women, the next objective, making the commitment last for a lifetime, is even more important.

Let's acknowledge a difficult truth. Many men stray from their marital partnership at one time or another. I strongly believe that if women have a healthier understanding of why men digress, they will be better equipped to prevent it from happening in their own marriages. In most cases it is possible to turn the tables with intelligence and planning. Once you understand why men stray, and what your special man's needs are, you can follow a simple proven approach that will support your man's desire to stay committed to you. That is the key, of course: helping the man himself to feel inspired to stay committed to the relationship. Here's another, perhaps surprising, truth: most men are as reluctant as women to throw away a long-term relationship. They are willing to heal—if their partners are.

I hope this book will inspire you to take a close look at your intimate relationship before it's too late. It will not suggest cute tricks, like greeting your husband at day's end wrapped in clear plastic wrap, nor does it suggest that you ignore your own needs in favor of his. It shows you how, through honest communication, motivation and problem-solving strategies—as well as by paying attention to a man's physical and emotional needs—you can sustain the commitment from the man you've chosen as your spouse. The purpose of this book is to help you better understand men and their thought processes—at least as they apply to their long-term commitments—thus strengthening your marriage and preventing divorce.

In my previous book I explored the reasons men are willing to commit to a particular relationship. I encouraged women to act as intelligently in their romances as they did in the rest of their lives, and showed how a businesslike approach to relationships could help them get what they wanted.

Why Men Stray, Why Men Stay is the logical extension of the program set out in *Why Men Commit*. The commitment process is only the first step in a lasting relationship, and your efforts should in no way end at that point. Successful businesspeople know that making and closing a sale is only the beginning of the process. They look to develop a long-term relationship with a client, one that will be rewarding and satisfying to both parties. They work hard at improving their connection with the client. I will show you how these same principles can also work in maintaining a long and mutually satisfying marriage.

A close correlation exists between managing personal and professional relationships. Both doing your job well and dealing with your personal life require you to learn what other people want—and devise ways to give them what they need. This very businesslike concept easily transfers to your personal relationships with men. This book shows you how to apply the same tactics you'd use in business—taking a proven, intellectual approach, developing a strategy, and applying it to your own ends in the relationship of your choice, leading to a lasting, rewarding commitment from your man.

What if your marriage is already in trouble . . . if you suspect, or know, that your partner is having an affair? If your marital relationship is not progressing to your satisfaction, you will learn how to turn the situation around before it becomes a permanent condition. I will show you how it's possible to put a temporarily floundering partnership back on the path to commitment.

This book offers a clear view of the complexities, misconceptions, issues, and myths women confront when they cross the border from the romantic illusion of marital bliss to the reality of married life. It suggests a practical ten-step marriage maintenance plan that anyone can use at any stage of a long-term relationship. It illustrates how through self-awareness and a few minor changes in your behaviors, you can keep your man committed to you forever. Your victory lies in making the commitment last, by making your man *want* to stay, rather than stray.

Read this book on your way to work; give it to your friends, your sister, your daughter, or mother. It will have a significant and positive impact on how you view your intimate relationships and your chances of success in keeping your man happily committed to you.

PART ONE

Why Men Stray

CHAPTER ONE

Dangerous Domain

*When he is late for dinner and I know he must be either
having an affair or lying dead in the street, I always hope
he's dead.*

☞ JUDITH VIORST

DIVORCE IS STILL EPIDEMIC IN AMERICA, but the direction in the
nineties is toward people trying to make their marriages last.
Although there are many valid reasons for divorce, adultery being
one of the most common, working on a relationship has become a
necessary exercise.

Men and women want to know how to heal and recover; they
are less willing to junk a long-term relationship. This is partly due to
the devastating effects divorce has on everyone involved. Most
people still suffer a severe income drop after divorce. Children suffer
emotionally. As marriages should not be entered into lightly, they
should also not be dissolved lightly. The throwaway marriage and
quickie divorce are things of the past.

You married for the rest of your life. It started out wonderfully,
but it doesn't stay that way without work. The purpose of this book is

3

to show you how to keep your man committed to you forever. By using the same logic and common sense that you used to work your way to a permanent commitment, you can follow a simple, proven strategy that will keep your relationship on the right track and sustain your man's desire to *stay* rather than *stray*.

In business you periodically re-evaluate your job responsibilities, discuss personal and team goals and long-term strategy. This same application is essential in a marriage. You signed a contract and marriage is a serious business. You don't want to be the intelligent woman who is successful in every other aspect of her life but checks her brain at the office door on Friday night. You picked up this book because you care and you want your marriage to be a success.

EXPECTATIONS

Many people marry without ever discussing their expectations of marriage, and may never discuss them. Others discuss what their expectations are at seventeen or twenty, but never keep themselves updated and negotiate as they age or as children are born or as they change jobs. You might have different expectations of your twenty-year-old husband who hasn't graduated from college yet than you do of your forty-year-old husband with a significant income and three kids. There's a big gap there. Expectations may change after children are born. The same is true for men. A man may have a different expectation of his young wife than he has of a mature woman who's now the mother of his children. Part of the success formula is making sure both partners are clear about where the other is coming from. This encompasses values and norms, shared perceptions and problem-solving strategies. Many marriages fail because of confused expectations.

Who were your role models growing up? Were they your parents, sitcom families, or families you read about in newspapers and magazines? Which models impressed you and affected your expectations? Perhaps your husband grew up watching the classic family TV shows of the fifties and sixties which featured women who stayed home with the kids and baked cookies. If his family situation was similar, this could be his comfort in our ever-changing world of working women and day care. He could be very uncomfortable with life in the nineties.

> *Love is not enough. It must be the foundation, the cornerstone—but not the complete structure. It is much too pliable, too yielding.*
>
> ⌒ BETTE DAVIS

THE MARRIAGE CULTURE

The transition from individualism to team effort is not an easy one. Problems occur when conflicting values and assumptions arise. Perhaps you came from a background different from that of your spouse and the transition has been less than optimal. A marriage is like no other relationship. It needs to find its shape and set its own rules. There needs to be a mutual understanding of what is going on both physically and emotionally. You need to be a good match for each other. Ideally, the marriage should turn out to be what you both want and thought you were getting into. Problems need to be addressed as they arise rather than saved up for an unrelated explosion.

Marriage is not ownership; it is coexistence. It's trust and living together and sharing dreams. No human being is owned by another. A wife isn't owned by a husband, and a husband isn't owned by a wife. Once you begin to look at your spouse as a possession—

someone who should live according to your rules and expectations—then you rob yourself of the joy of a mutually loving, supporting, respecting relationship.

Everybody comes with some kind of baggage—whether it's family or children or debt, an aging, dependent parent, or an inability to be organized or to problem-solve. Everyone has problems and faults, and you just have to buy into the whole package and deal with them. You need to recognize that one person is not all things to another. It's not possible. The things that you don't get from your spouse, whatever they may be, you have to find elsewhere. And this is not, and should not seem, threatening.

Marriage is probably the most difficult situation in which you will ever find yourself. Nobody has a fifty-year plan for anything. Even in business, you may have a ten-year plan that you present to investors. If it works, they're so impressed that you get the promotion, and eventually you become CEO. Society expects you to find a partner when you're about twenty years old and successfully live with that person for fifty years. And if you don't, you're judged a failure. This is totally unrealistic because people change, and you need to realize that, in order for a marriage to last, it's probably going to be the hardest work you will encounter in your life.

The proprietary aspect is always complex. Suppose someone comes up at a social event and flirts with your husband. You get angry at him, and that puts him on the defensive because he hasn't done anything. He gets mad at you. One of the wonderful things in life is innocent flirtation. Nothing is going to come of it unless there's something missing in your relationship. If that should be the case, you must address it. Put yourself in your husband's position—if he started to make accusations, you wouldn't like it. You can't tell another person what to do, because you do not own him.

Regardless of all the difficulties and the high divorce rate, marriage is alive and well in the nineties. Be it the traditional marriage with the stereotypical role of man as the head of household and the at-home wife, or a more modern version with both partners sharing in the earning and the household chores, or any combination or change, it's still here. We all want to know how and why some of these partnerships are more successful and happier than others.

The following pages will provide you with some insight into what works, what doesn't, what can go wrong, and how, through developing your own plan, positive change is possible.

LOU, LOOKING FOR NUMBER THREE:

"My second wife had so much baggage,
she needed her own redcap."

❦ ❦ ❦

I was introduced to a woman recently who sadly related the story of how her husband of thirty-two years had just left her. She had seen me on several TV talk shows as the "commitment expert" and thought that perhaps I could give her some insight into why this had happened to her. She claimed total naiveté and shock.

"How could he do this to me after all I've been through?" she asked. "I've nursed him back to health, and he turns around and leaves me."

"Didn't you have a feeling that things were not going well?" I asked, thinking that I would certainly have picked up on a domestic problem way before this point. Was there no communication? Beverly was distraught. She'd lost forty pounds on the "divorce diet" (which she liked), but she'd also lost most of her hair, and she was wearing a wig. As I listened to her, the problems became apparent. I couldn't help thinking that this was an all-too-familiar story.

Unfortunately, Beverly had ceased paying attention to her spouse or her relationship for quite some time. After her children were grown and out of the house, she buried herself in tennis and community volunteering. She went on junkets with women friends and no longer made the effort to vacation with her husband or accompany him on business trips. She had drifted very far from her partner without realizing it. Life went along status quo until a shock jilted Beverly and her husband into reality.

Edward was diagnosed with cancer and thought he would not live. Beverly stuck by his side and nurtured him back to health. When he was feeling confident that he'd beaten his illness, he divorced Beverly for a younger woman. The way Edward sees it, he was given a second chance at happiness and at life itself. He seized the opportunity.

He had a health crisis and decided that he wanted to be free, to have fun, and above all, he wanted love. For too many years he and Beverly had been going through the motions of a relationship but had long since fallen out of touch with each other. They hadn't slept together in years, she assumed by mutual agreement, since Edward had not verbalized any complaints. She suspected several affairs during their married life but never said anything. She feels very betrayed now that he left her because she put up with the "deal" all those years. He no longer felt romantically inclined toward her and resented the mother role she had taken on during his recovery.

Had Beverly periodically re-evaluated her relationship and made the effort to be more communicative and spend more time with her husband, this problem might have been avoided.

How wonderful to have someone to blame! How won-derful to live with one's nemesis! You may be miserable, but you feel forever in the right. You may be fragmented, but you feel absolved of all the blame for it.

⌐ ERIKA JONG

Amy, thirty-nine, married for twelve years, mother of three young children, was stunned when her husband suddenly left her and moved in with another woman.

"He says he's in love with her!" Amy went on to say that Hank, forty-four, had been having a midlife crisis since he'd turned forty. "He was the least likely person to ever do anything like this," she said, bewildered.

Amy's husband, Hank, was anxious to give his side of the story after a little persuasion on my part. I too was surprised by his behavior and convinced him that what he had to say might be helpful to other women. Here's what he said, in its entirety. It summarizes what, for many men, covers similar marital frustrations. Hank presents himself as a *stayer* who strayed.

HANK, INVESTMENT COUNSELOR, SAYS:

"I was married for twelve years and I do equate marriage with monogamy. I never strayed until now. The reason I strayed is complicated, but at the time it felt pretty simple. The core of the incentive to stray was the dysfunctional nature of the sexual relationship with my wife, Amy. When I met Janet (the strayee), it was just a fluke. She was somebody that I had a lot in common with, and the opportunity was there.

"Years ago, when I lived in New York, I was around women all the time at work. I worked downtown on Wall Street, and I had a lot of female friends and unbelievable opportunities to be unfaithful, and I never once was. It was almost ridiculous. Most of the women were younger than I was, two or three years out of college. I had a reputation for not straying, and they hit on me for that very reason. I never strayed under those circumstances. We didn't have any kids when we moved to Connecticut ten years ago and we started our family. I worked at home, and we had three kids fast. I wasn't around a lot of women. I don't go bar hopping, and I don't go out with the guys.

"My wife knew there was a significant problem. She's not a very sexual person. When we were young and single and had kind of independent lives, she was working, I was working, and it was just a different relationship. Sex was more of an accommodation to me. I didn't realize it at the time. As I got older and more sophisticated, I wanted more out of the relationship, but at the same time, we were having kids, and instead of there being five reasons for not being in bed together, there were a hundred. And a hundred good ones! When you've got kids, there are concerns with them and a lot is going on. If the other person doesn't want to accommodate you, it's pretty easy for her to put you in a position where you're imposing or not being sensitive. So it just spiraled downward.

"Being in my early forties and having changes in my own sexual functioning, I thought I was impotent. My sexual interest went to zero. With the combination of that and age, I thought I was finished. I was ripe for the picking, believe me. That happens a lot with men who have been in long relationships— they're in midlife and things are pretty dead sexually between them and their wives, and then all of a sudden that right woman comes along and says the right things, and all of a sudden he feels like he's seventeen again. It's like a rebirth, and let me tell you, I don't care what's at stake with a man, if it's kids or money. If that rebirth occurs, it's almost impossible for him to give it up.

"The nice guy who started out in the marriage as number one becomes more of a doormat over the years. It's like you're friends and she counts on you and takes you for granted. Unfortunately, the guys who are the most committed, the most dependable, get dumped on the most. The guys who are my age, who cheat all the time, have wives who are all over them because they're afraid he's going to stray. It keeps them on edge. There's a feeling that they have to compete for his attention even though they've been married all those years, and it drives the relationship. It seems like you need conflict for progress. That conflict between men and women is at the very root of our being. I think you can overcome it, but it takes a lot of savvy on the part of women.

"I think there's this great gulf between men and women in the genetic material. Because we're so highly political in this country with the women's movement, there is the idea that this is a learned behavior. The conduct that men exhibit is in the genetic code. Women are more complicated—they're not as easily satisfied.

"Men stray because of sex. As they get older, they'll be less likely to stray. At a certain point men and women become emotionally more compatible as they age. Agendas change, sex drives drop, and men, because of experience and a little more wisdom, have a tendency to be more receptive to a female approach to things.

"I think that relationships are vulnerable at different times. Friends I had in New York in my twenties and thirties didn't talk about this. Men my age are talking about it because they have a lot in common. They've been in long-term relationships, and they feel vulnerable for reasons that are obvious. They're opening up, so I've learned a lot. I never had these conversations with male friends when I was younger. We were programmed not to discuss these things. I've been in the dark most of my life. I've taken an interest in the subject now because I have friends talking to me and because of my personal experience. I feel I have some real insights into relationships now: men are more basic and women more complicated.

"I don't know about a long-term relationship between two young people without a wealth of knowledge and experience, but who plan the traditional 'getting married and having a family and being together forever.' For there to be any chance for that relationship to be healthy, successful, and long lasting, there has to be a great sexual relationship, absolutely no question about it! And that's very rare. I don't feel it's a situation where women should feel they have to accommodate. That won't work for any length of time. The unfortunate thing about sexuality is that it's learned behavior. Human beings have sex in private, they don't talk about it. In surveys people often lie about their behavior. Sex really is a very involved, intricate behavior that has to be learned, and we don't teach it. I think for women to be successful with men over a long period, they have to focus a great deal on their own sexuality and have the male experience that with them. A woman has to create great love, but in order to do that she has to be in tune with her own sexuality. If he can duplicate the experience by picking someone up in a bar at any time, that's not going to work—men have a natural inclination toward variety. So it isn't just being a good performer in a very basic way—that won't work because it's human nature to lose interest. It has to go beyond that. There has to be an emotional quality to the sexuality, and that's really a woman's nature—it isn't a man's nature, but he can learn it. Once that emotional bond has been tied to the sexuality between a man and a woman, he can't duplicate it with a casual affair. There's just something about true sexual intimacy that you can't fake. There's nothing more attractive to a man than a woman who really enjoys sex. No man is going to want to put that at risk, so he will curb his behavior."

☙ ☙ ☙

Hank and Amy seemed to be a sexual mismatch from the beginning, which escalated over time. If they had re-evaluated their expectations of each other and of the relationship, if she had made the effort to awaken her sexuality and reclaim her sensual self, he probably would have stayed. Who knows? She might have actually enjoyed herself.

Hank's story is typical of why so many men stray. He became the forgotten "nice guy." His wife took him for granted and assumed she could ignore his needs. She neglected to service the account, so he took his business elsewhere.

Time and again we hear similar stories of women like Beverly and Amy, who thought they were happily married, only to have the rug pulled out from under them. Were there signs that they'd missed, or had they just shut down and closed themselves off from any communication with their partners?

Is it possible to marry for all the right reasons, think you are happy, and then just have everything explode in your face? Unfortunately, the answer is yes. A relationship, like anything else, requires constant maintenance and reassessment to make sure it's kept in working order. If taken for granted, it could die slowly, without the conscious awareness of either party, even though you thought it was for the rest of your life.

The potential for enjoying a successful marriage already exists within you if you have chosen the right man. By approaching your relationship with logic and common sense as well as emotion, you can put yourself more in control of the course your love life takes. A sense of humor can be an invaluable tool.

Husbands are like fires. They go out when unattended.

☞ Zsa Zsa Gabor

Should This Marriage Be Saved?

More than half of American marriages end in divorce. Which 50 percent do you want to end up in? How much do you want to work to save the union, and is it worth it? Only you can decide. As an adult, you must take responsibility for your own life and personal happiness. You cannot and should not look to your spouse to fulfill your sense of self, nor should you focus on blame at this point. Tell yourself, "I am not happy, so I will do this" rather than adopt the victim's approach: "He did this" or "He doesn't make me happy." It's your life, and you are in charge.

If you've read this far and think you may not want to put forth the effort, you probably shouldn't. Of course, if Jack Nicholson or Prince Charles is your husband's role model, there's little hope. Forget blame. Just try to discern if the mistakes you've made could have been avoided, so you don't make the same mistakes again. Take responsibility for yourself and make the decision. If you want him to stay, then keep that as your main focus and put together a plan to make it work.

Perhaps there are fundamental differences and a power struggle is always at play. Weigh your man's merits; is it likely that you can turn things around? You can't force an issue. You have to know when to dismiss him and go on with your life. Carefully evaluate what's happened in your relationship, and if there was an error on your part, make certain you don't make the same mistake again. You are the important person here. You need to get on with your life and goals, either with your spouse or without him.

Most women I talked to said that they could forgive their spouse one mistake, but they could not deal with a pattern of straying. For our purposes, though, a man can have a long-running affair, serial affairs, or an occasional fling, and he qualifies for the *strayer* category. He may leave the relationship permanently, or he may choose to stray *and* stay. This is the most frustrating and damaging of situations. The wife keeps hoping he will change and wondering every time he walks out the door if he's really going where he says he's going. So the trust goes down the drain. It's like the dog that suddenly bites you—do you ever really trust that dog again?

Straying is a symptom, not any one pattern or habit. Some marriages last forever despite the fact that the man may have these little flings along the way. Maybe that's okay with you. You have to decide if you want to keep him around. Does he stray every weekend, or once every five years? Is he a salesman who goes to a convention in Las Vegas once a year and goes crazy? Perhaps you think it's harmless and you can live with it. Maybe you are afraid of contracting the dreaded AIDS. This may sound morbid, but it definitely factors into the equation in the nineties.

If you're reading this, you probably want to make the effort to end the straying. You can! Recognizing and admitting that there is an issue is an important step in understanding a problem that has many facets. Most men who talked to me said they wanted an emotional copilot, and reacted, after mature consideration, in a negative way to wives who tried to own or control them.

CHAPTER TWO

The Whens and Whys
of Straying

STRAY *intr. v.* To wander from a given place or group or beyond established limits; roam. To become lost. To deviate from a course that is regarded as right or moral; go astray. To deviate from the subject matter at hand; digress. *n.* One that has strayed; especially, a domestic animal at large or lost.

❦ ❦ ❦

MEN STRAY BECAUSE THEY CAN. The human being is an animal who has certain inherited physical and emotional traits, capacities, and limitations. (And, make no mistake about it, men are sexual beings.) The woman who takes her man to nirvana and keeps him happy and satisfied will be the winner. She holds the key. Everything else is secondary.

Part of straying is cognitive and psychological to the extent that it's an expression of interest outside everyday life. It's a form of excitement, of titillation above and beyond the normal. It's not like going on "Space Mountain," but it's excitement to the extent that you derive a pleasure and a newness from something. In part, it comes from yourself and in part from the other person. Boredom is a big part of it. The old saying "An idle mind is the devil's workshop" has relevance here. The woman who stays home with the kids for five years could become boring. You may not have much to talk about if all you have are your utilitarian jobs and TV. It's essential to develop the ability to occupy yourself in a useful way and still feel like a human being, even if you're at home with the kids.

WHEN MEN STRAY

There are many times when men are more vulnerable to straying. These are the instances when you have to be especially careful:

- When the wife is pregnant
- When he has survived a long-term illness or an accident
- When he travels
- In midlife
- When he completes an academic degree
- After an "up" like a promotion—career success
- When he's drunk or high from substance abuse
- When the wife returns to work (less attention for him)
- When he's bored

WHYS

Why They Say They Stray

MICHAEL, SECOND MARRIAGE:

"There are only two reasons for straying: (1)You don't like what you do have, or (2)You do like what you don't have."

❦   ❦   ❦

1. Not sexually satisfied at home/"Bad sex"
2. Boredom
3. A need for adventure: "The challenge (to see if I can get away with it)"
4. Emotional claustrophobia at home
5. Not enough attention from spouse: "My wife was always too busy; I needed to share dinner with someone"
6. Lack of communication
7. "She let herself go"
8. "I was never in love in the first place!"

There are almost as many reasons to stray as there are men. But the same themes come up again and again. Here's what men say about the most common reasons that they stray.

Familiarity

PAUL, FIFTY-ONE, MARRIED A VERY LONG TIME:

"The problem with being married for a very long time is that
you can become like brother and sister! Above all, you've got to
keep the excitement."

☙   ☙   ☙

He will stray when he's unhappy at home, dissatisfied at work, or because he's threatened by the idea of his youth slipping away. He may stray after a life-threatening illness, when he has been confronted by his own mortality. One of the more painful times for women to deal with is when they are betrayed after they have been the backbone of support, either assisting in putting him through school, or helping him climb the corporate ladder in his business. It's as if he has the wings to fly away now, just as a grown, educated child would. He thinks it's time to move on. The woman is particularly upset because after all her effort and labor, she doesn't get to experience the power, prestige, and money that she worked so hard to attain for both of them.

Availability

If your work or his has led to your spending long periods away from each other, then the unavoidable result could be an affair. If one or both partners are so busy that they feel they have to make an appointment to see each other, then any woman who's available and pays attention to him starts to look good.

Adventure and Risk

Never underestimate man's need for adventure. This is mainly the reason for a one-night stand. He wants to see if he can get away with it. He's immature and feels trapped. Mark, a twenty-three-year-old painter, says, "I wasn't ready for marriage. I was too young."

Sexual Excitement of Another Woman

Everyone loves the dance—the excitement, the thrill, the romance of someone new. Wouldn't you like someone to pick you up, give you flowers, tell you how wonderful you are and hang on every word you say? Seduction—who doesn't love that? The best part of straying is the dance. Gilbert, a forty-six-year-old strayer, says, "Everyone loves the dance of romance. I missed the dance."

Ego Reinforcement and Attention

Guys tell the worst jokes; they want someone to laugh at them. The wife says, "I've heard that joke fifteen times." She rolls her eyes and changes the subject. His feelings are hurt.

In defense of his relationship with twenty-four-year-old Soon-Yi Previn, Woody Allen, fifty-nine, recently said, "She's a marvel. And she laughs at all my jokes."

Money

Never underestimate the role finances can play in any love match. The financial situation could destroy the relationship altogether. Financial pressures are responsible for many divorces. Money can be a crucial concern, especially if a man is unemployed or paying alimony and/or child support. A spendaholic wife creates undue pressure. Alan, now divorced, says, "It's not unusual for a married guy with a family to think of himself as only the 'meal ticket.' Nobody appreciates me except for the fact that I have money and pay all the bills and take them places. I just want to find someone who values me for being me."

Shift of Focus

The wife has shifted her concentration from her spouse to the kids, to her job, or to other activities, leaving him feeling unimportant and with a hurt ego. He doesn't get enough attention, so he's not happy. He wants it the way it used to be.

Make a concentrated effort not to focus all of your attention on your newborn or other children, thereby neglecting your husband. Many men complain that the companionship is not what it used to be, and that their wives spend too much time with the kids. This is among the most common reasons for men straying.

Sam, a thirty-four-year-old strayer, says, "I married my wife because I loved her and she was my best friend and favorite companion. We had two children. One has attention-deficit disorder. She is obsessed with this child, taking him to classes and different specialists. She won't leave him with a baby-sitter, so we never go out.

She's running here and there, trying to be Mother of the Year. I don't mean to trivialize what she's doing, but I think she's putting too much pressure on the kid, and he'd be better off without all the attention. I moved out and am living with someone who has a little time for me. Now my wife is taking me to court and trying to get more money out of me. Someday, my son will grow up and move out, and she will be lost."

Appearance

Physical attraction is a significant part of any marriage, but most men aren't looking for beauty queens. A pleasing overall appearance based on the individual's own aesthetic is what men find important in the commitment process. It's important to stay within the range that initially attracted him if you want him to stay at home. I'm not talking about the natural aging process. But drastic changes, such as a considerable weight gain, are a big turn-off. As Erik, a thirty-eight-year-old architect, said of his wife, "She used to be really well put together. She chose her clothing more carefully. Now that she has gained weight, she let herself go. She just doesn't turn me on anymore."

JOSEPH, TWICE DIVORCED:

"A ring on the finger is a license to eat. Both of my wives
gained a lot of weight and that was a big turn-off!"

🌿 🌿 🌿

Common Interests

It's important to find the right balance in a relationship, and sometimes that means actively trying to do things together. It's okay to have different hobbies and friends, but you've also got to have interests that you share. The companionship needs to be maintained. The older we get, the less we like to compromise, but if you want the relationship to work out, it's necessary to expand. Take a chance; you might enjoy the challenge of doing something new, and you might even be better at it than he is. If you play, he will stay! As Drake, a fifty-five-year-old retired executive, says, "I love to play golf every other day. At my age I'm attracted to someone who likes to do the things that I like to do."

Midlife Crisis

He's in serious need of reinforcement. You just have to be supportive of him and make him feel young and sexy. You could help him explore new things. Maybe he'll get over it. John, forty-two, now separated, says, "It was hard for me to realize that I was at the top of the hill and the only way to go was down. I guess I thought an affair would help slow the ride."

Revenge

How better to get back at you for your infidelity than fighting fire with fire? As Morty sophomorically stated, "She started it! What goes around comes around."

The Aging Ego

His wife takes him for granted; she may be busy with organizations, card groups, her children or grandchildren. They have grown in different directions. He needs the reinforcement of youthful attention. David, age fifty-eight, said, "A lot of women find me fascinating because I'm older. I know how to go into a restaurant and order a nice bottle of wine, and it even has a cork in it. I drive a Mercedes."

Travel

If one of you travels a good bit of the time, he will seek attention where he can. Remember the song, "If you can't be with the one you love, love the one you're with." As Lee, a thirty-six-year-old-musician says, "A good shack away is as satisfying as a great take-out meal."

Monotony

Men will stray when they're in a rut. If it seems to him that all he does is work and take care of the kids and tend to monotonous day-to-day business, he'll feel trapped. Any diversion would be gratefully accepted. J. T., aged forty-one, says, "Life speeds along—work and the kids don't leave time for a life. I long for the past days of freedom. Now I don't feel so bad about squandering my youth—booze, drugs, and indiscriminate sex sound like more fun than most of what I do these days."

This does not necessarily mean the end of the relationship. He could actually be happily married but tired of the same old thing. All the menial chores of the day can push the two of you into obsessing and talking about little else. Guess what? It's boring and it's not sexually stimulating; your husband doesn't want to get bogged down in the tedium of everyday life. Jack, married for sixteen years, says, "She's no longer interesting. When we dated, she had a job and money and something to talk about."

Loss of Control

Men don't like controlling, bossy women. They want a partner, not a mother. Don't dictate; learn how to make a suggestion.

ADAM, MARRIED TWENTY-TWO YEARS, NOW SEPARATED, SAYS:

"At one point I just said, 'I've had enough! This woman is not going to dictate to me what I can spend on myself.' It's more than sexual; I had a great thing on the side, and yet I would cringe when Carolyn walked into the room because it would be another, 'You can't do this' or 'We have to do that,' 'We're going here' or 'We're doing this!' The decision making on every level was taken out of my hands. I'm not a child, and I don't want to be treated like one.

"If I said I wanted it to be a team decision, it would escalate into a fight. A fight does not lead to sitting down and having a discussion. My wife was run by money—it was the main thing. It's a dangerous trap to get into.

"There are kids and finances and elements to deal with. Men are fairly simple. We're not asking for all that much. The older we get, affection gets to be equally important as sex. General attention is very important.

"When the emotions went, the sex life went with it. If I can't stand to be in the same room with someone, I certainly don't want to fuck them. Sex becomes the major thing."

❦ ❦ ❦

MATT, THIRTY-EIGHT, ACTOR, SAYS:

"If you're with an emotionally disturbed woman, you're already in trouble. You don't always know that until you're already hooked. I don't mean just PMS. The need to control comes out of being emotionally disturbed. If a woman doesn't trust you, she's going to try to control you. If she tries to control you, you're going to stray eventually. If a woman depends on you for her happiness, you're going to stray because you feel like you're in a box and you can't wait to get out. It's like being involved with an emotional vampire.

"Let me give you an example of a controlling woman. Someone who calls every night to make sure you're home at a certain time and, if you're not, thinks you're out screwing around. Someone who listens to every story and believes the worst about you. Someone who's out to prove that you're going to desert her because that's the story she's written for herself. She's afraid of losing you so she tries to control you to keep you from going. It's a never-ending saga, and it's a disaster no matter how you look at it. It's true for men and women, that if you don't have any kind of center within yourself, and if you're dependent on another person for your happiness, it's not going to work. You've heard all the clichés, but they happen to be true. Looking for a man to make you happy is a trap.

"My advice is that if a woman is fulfilled by her own life, that's going to radiate in a relationship and a man is not going to want to stray. You can trust a woman like that. If a woman is really needy, by my experience, that means if you're not there for her, she's going to want to find something to fill the empty space in her, because it's a black hole that can never be filled. It's like a woman who uses marriage as a threat: 'If you don't marry me, then I'm going to do *this*.' Well, if everything was working right for her, I'd want to marry her.

"You could be a housewife and be independent. You need to realize that a marriage or a relationship isn't going to be the thing that makes your life work. If you go into it thinking that's going to make you completely happy, you're in for a disappointment. We all want to share life and intimacy with someone and have fun together. I strayed because my wife was very needy and therefore incredibly destructive. She was manipulative and played games. Once you get into that, it's a war.

"The couples that I see make it work all trust each other. There's a whole other dimension here that I don't know about. And after twenty years of marriage, people can still be sexually hot for each other.

"On a certain level a man can separate sex from intimacy. If a man wants to get laid, he can go—boom—got laid, see ya later. Young, dumb, and full of come!

"I'm out for good, but I'm trying to understand it. It was familiar. If a dog sleeps on a rusty nail long enough, it doesn't know it's sleeping on a rusty nail. We're all romantic and we all get fucked over by the idea of romantic love—we will all go for it and get burned by it no matter what. I think everybody gets burned by romantic love because it's an unrealistic expectation. I'm defining romantic love as a love where you think that the other person's going to do it or solve it or make your life happy, and that's not possible if you're not happy yourself. The expectation is just too high. I find that some women have a very romantic and unrealistic view of wanting to get married when they reach a certain age. They just want to get married for the security or the biological clock, but it makes for a disastrous recipe."

　　　　🌾　　🌾　　🌾

In survey results of over one thousand married men, 79 percent of them said they committed because of love, companionship, and great sex. A man marries with the right intentions, and he wants it to work. The commitment process breaks down when one or more of these elements is removed from his relationship. Did he change, or did you?

The typical man marries his best friend, with whom he likes to have sex. The overwhelming majority of men I spoke to rated sexual fulfillment as a very important factor in committing to marriage. A satisfying sexual relationship makes a man feel important and strengthens his self-confidence. A good many men commit primarily because a regular sex partner is important. Most men I interviewed said that the best lover is a woman who responds to and enjoys sex herself. It should come as no surprise, then, to find out that sex is the single biggest reason men stray. Either they don't get enough at home, or it's boring.

Many women get so caught up in feelings of betrayal that they don't examine what motivates their man to stray from his commitment. Is it the need for excitement, or is it a complex set of forces, that result in his dalliances? But this is not about blame. You will need to make the effort to understand his behavior with all of its complexities and contradictions. We want to know how our spouse thinks and feels if we are to develop a plan and alleviate the problem.

It's been said that all men stray at one time or another. However, these conceptions are based on tacit assumptions about what motivates men to stray. These are generalizations about men, and in reality each man must be considered individually.

Spouses who are frequently separated have a higher stray rate. We need to look no farther than Hollywood, where one partner is off on location for a minimum of three months, to know this is true. Spouses often stray with their costars. As Emma Thompson said in announcing her recent divorce from actor Kenneth Branagh, "Our work has inevitably led to our spending long periods away from each other, and, as a result, we have drifted apart."

JIMMY, AGE FIFTY-FOUR, TRUCK DRIVER,
MARRIED THIRTY-THREE YEARS:

"The way I see it, there are three stages of sex, and we are in the third. The first stage is house sex. That's when you fuck in every room of the house—kitchen, living room, etcetera. The second stage is bedroom sex. You just fuck in the bedroom. Third stage is hallway sex. That's when you pass each other in the hallway and say, 'Go fuck yourself!' We're in the hallway phase of our marriage."

❦ ❦ ❦

Men who are happy and satisfied act differently from those who are unsatisfied.

Sociological, economic, psychological, and physical considerations make a difference in motivation and behavior. Men generally stray to fill a need that is lacking in their spousal relationship.

Straying is about dissatisfaction and unhappiness. In our society of instant gratification and happiness, as demonstrated in the media and with the commercials we watch, we ask ourselves, "Why can't I be happy?" We seek the happiness that the media tell us we deserve. So men stray. They may ask themselves, "Do I stay with what I know, or do I go with the excitement?"

If women only knew what really made their own men stray, they would feel more confident in their ability to prevent it from happening. They would have a better opportunity to create satisfying partnerships. It is imperative to develop a sophisticated understanding of what motivates your man in order to be able to deal with the situation and turn it around. Some sharp women have the ability to enter a new situation, size it up, and instinctively make the right moves. Most of us are not so blessed. We need training to become more skilled in dealing with men. We also need to learn more about ourselves. You can control your own behavior and you must assume responsibility for it, but you can't control his behavior. This is perhaps the most important principal. You must see yourself as the central point of control and change. You have to learn to cope with conflict and difficult situations. You need to understand his culture, ethics, values, and driving force, and, finally, you must develop the strategy to handle the situation effectively.

Did you choose the right man at the right time, or is this a case of a premature commitment backfiring? You may want to ask yourself what needs he is trying to satisfy, if you can fulfill those needs, and if you want to. Remember that your needs are also crucial.

Sex is so important it deserves a chapter of its own—read on.

CHAPTER THREE

You Guessed It—Sex

CHRIS, REMARRIED, FORMER STRAYER:

"Man's basic instinct is to get laid."

❦ ❦ ❦

OUR MEN ARE TEMPTED EVERY DAY of their lives. If he's someone you want to keep, then anticipate and understand the temptations and deal with them. Even if he's not actively looking, the barracudas are out there. Men like to be reassured that they're still attractive and sexy. When they get the attention of someone who catches them off guard, they like it and they're flattered.

Let's look at things from a man's viewpoint for a moment and examine their feelings more closely.

SEX

The pursuit of sexual satisfaction is the number-one reason men stray. The lack or infrequency of a sex life, or boredom with their wives, is why men look elsewhere. After all, they don't just want to *talk* to the other woman. Sexuality is also one of the most common areas that changes over time with women. The former single and sexually uninhibited woman, the woman going after the commitment, often changes with her marriage vows, due to career, to family responsibilities, or to sheer exhaustion. Perhaps she loses interest after her family is complete. Or, with hormonal shifts after childbearing or menopause, the libido decreases. Sex may drop to the bottom of her priority list. Guess what? It's almost always right up there, vying for first place, on the man's list. If his wife is not available or if she is not interested, he'll find someone who is.

BEN, THIRD MARRIAGE, STAYER:

"My second wife didn't believe in oral sex—
either coming or going!"

❦ ❦ ❦

The stimulation issue is fundamental. Do you enjoy doing things together? People are happier if they have interests other than themselves and the basics of clothing and feeding themselves and having sex. Those whose basic needs aren't being met seek gratification through stimulation, which in your spouse's case may end up being "bars, beer and broads." So your man can fulfill his basic needs with an affair. It's been legitimized—you see it as acceptable on TV and in the media. It's a recurring theme—the old boys' network. Women having affairs is considered subversive, whereas men having affairs draws a much wider variety of reactions.

Women control sex. Women control when men are going to have sex and when they're not. Unless a man is gay, he strays with women. There is no shortage of available and willing women who are not concerned about hurting their "sisters." This, coupled with the fact that men are expected to take advantage of any opportunity for sex or face ridicule, is why they stray. A weak man may not think he has a choice in the face of temptation.

And then, through no fault of his own and when he least expects it—Sexual Chemistry 101. He's happily married, and a woman appears. Sweaty palms, rapid heartbeat; his eyes lock with hers and he is flooded with emotion. Natural chemistry poses a danger even when he's not actively in the market for an affair. It's the thrill of the attraction, the flirting that follows. It's animal magnetism, and it's tough to turn down if she is aggressive.

Men are high maintenance. In the event that they are not getting all the attention they need, for whatever reason, they will seek it elsewhere—and find it. He may think an affair is the cure-all to any of the problems mentioned in the previous chapter. Man's strongest urge is to procreate the race. There is no limit as to how many times a man can have sex theoretically, within human limits. A woman is pregnant for nine months; she's done her thing and she is going to have a child. The man has no such boundaries. So perhaps the desire to have sex is not so strong in women during pregnancy. This may also be the case for women who have completed their families. They see no further reason for sex, or they may fear unwanted pregnancies. As difficult as this is to deal with, it's important to be aware of the fact and discuss it ahead of time. Forewarned is forearmed. After all, someone's got to put the happy in "Mr. Happy," and if it's not you, it will be somebody else.

As you will find out from reading the stories that follow, men stray at different times in their lives, and for very different reasons.

> *Oh, life is a glorious cycle of song,*
> *A medley of extemporanea;*
> *And love is a thing that can never go wrong;*
> *And I am Marie of Roumania.*

> ⇝ DOROTHY PARKER

DONALD, FIFTY-ONE, DIVORCED AND REMARRIED, SAYS:

"There is no solution. Given the opportunity, there's probably 1 percent of the population that wouldn't fuck around. Men stray because they're men. That's about as simple as you can get. It's the culture of the penis, and that is where men live.

"I had a friend who played in a rock band. He fucked about four women a night. He's a singer, and there are all these women who want to be with him; what's he going to say, no? More men screw around than don't. They like the sport of it. It's fun. The sixties changed everything. Men became the pursued.

"American women are puritanical—every other culture is more understanding. If you think you're going to marry someone outgoing and charming, and you're attracted to him for the same reasons everyone else is, and you think he's going to change when you get married, that's ludicrous. In my twenties, thirties, and forties, nothing was going to stop me. I worked in sales and I traveled a lot. I worked for guys like me. My trainer in sales, a vice president of my training program in the seventies, said that the only good salesmen are the guys who love sex. He said, 'I don't want a guy working for me that doesn't love sex because he's not going to be a good salesman.' You have to have confidence. Part of it is the chase. Prospect, qualify, and close. He said that if a man doesn't have a great sex drive, he's going to be a lousy salesman. An accountant doesn't screw around.

"Men and women are basically very different. The sexual revolution died real fast because women aren't really promiscuous. Women go through periods where they might try it for a year or two and screw around, but then they change."

🌾 🌾 🌾

WALTER, FIFTY-TWO, MARRIED THIRTY-TWO YEARS, SAYS:

"Men stray because they like variety. They think with their penises. Women think with their heads and their hearts. They like the emotional bond and they need that love. To them it's love. To men it's sex—and that's the difference. That's why men stray. Men feel that they need the variety and they love the new sex. I think that the general population of women doesn't love sex. They love it when they have sex with somebody they love; they feel a bond. Men can do it with anybody; it doesn't matter."

❦ ❦ ❦

A man may stray when his wife is pregnant, for lack of attention, or because he married young and never had the opportunity to "sow his oats."

The following story illustrates a combination of the two.

DOROTHY, AGE FIFTY-FIVE,
MARRIED TWENTY-FIVE YEARS, SAYS:

"I was happy—I thought everything was wonderful. I was married at thirty; my husband was twenty-seven. I was very experienced in life, from one-night stands to good times. I knew what life was all about, but my husband hadn't had the experiences I'd had. So all of a sudden he is going out and straying on me. We went to a psychiatrist at a friend's suggestion. I went because I loved him. I found out that my husband thought he couldn't compete with all the lovers I had had. So, of course, when these other girls came on to him, it was strictly an ego thing. I did not leave him over a piece of ass. I would never divorce my husband over that, which they were. He had one affair, which really hurt, but when I understood why he was doing it, it was up to me to try to correct the problem.

"Then I got pregnant. I could not have sex and was in the hospital for seven months. I found out that my husband was having an affair with one of my friends. Back to the psychiatrist. I couldn't have sex, but he had to have it. Pregnancy is a big time for men to screw around. If you can't take care of your husband, he will go elsewhere even though maybe there is a reason you can't. I have seen these gorgeous young boys come into a bar and pick up girls, and I would always ask them, 'Are you married, and is your wife pregnant? Why aren't you home with her?' They would answer, 'I've got to get relief.'

"There's oral sex, vibrators, hands. But when you're pregnant and huge up to your tonsils and feel lousy, oral sex is the furthest thing from your mind. We feel like we look ugly and not in the least sexy. You wonder how he could get turned on. He says, 'I'll go get a prostitute or a one-night stand,' and we forgive them—wrong!"

🌿 🌿 🌿

This was a sad case of miscommunication to begin with, and a lot of pain for Dorothy to work through. He was too young and inexperienced and saw the opportunity to make up for lost time when his wife was unavailable. Dorothy is still married and says she is happy they were able to work their problems out through counseling.

One primary reason men stray is that their sexual relationship with their wife changes after marriage.

PROFILE OF A TEMPORARY STRAYER

CARTER, THIRTY-THREE, LEGALLY SEPARATED; WITH HIS
WIFE TEN YEARS, MARRIED FIVE YEARS, SAYS:

"Before we were married, we partied quite a bit. And I don't mean just drinking. We grew to know each other under some strange circumstances. We used to watch porno movies together. When you party with some of the stuff we were partying on, like cocaine, sex comes pretty easily under the circumstances. When we stopped doing that kind of stuff, we had to rediscover ourselves. I never hid anything. I went to strip bars, too. I still go, because since we got married, my wife's not very sexual, but I am. I told her it was something we could try to work out, or she could let me read my magazines. Big deal! But she feels threatened. She used to crave me. It made me feel great!

"If I had one piece of advice to give to women, it would be that men like it a little crude. We like it when a woman acts a little coarse sexually and can be vocal about it. Women don't realize this, so they don't do it, and the man gets his crudeness through magazines or another woman. I buy the girlie magazines to look at the naked women. Men who say they're buying porno to read the articles—they're not. If I had a woman who would satisfy me, I wouldn't have to look at those magazines. It comes down to the fact that if you're not being satisfied, you look elsewhere. Women who don't like their husbands to read these magazines should be happy that they aren't looking for real women. They should sit down and figure out what their man's needs are. If he needs crudeness, then be crude for him. Is that asking so much? You can be compatible when you get married, like we were, and then somebody changes. If she has to get a little bit tipsy to be uninhibited, something's wrong."

🌱 🌱 🌱

Here's a case of different sexual styles and expectations between a husband and wife. What if she says, "But I want romance" or "It makes me feel dirty" or "Why should you look at other women and not look at me?" These are standard responses from women about men who want their sex "dirty."

The problem is that the men liked the sex the way it was before they married, but now that they're married, the women don't like to do it "that way" anymore. This is another way that women, not men, change. You may think that girlfriends can be sexy, but not wives. And mothers certainly can't, because sex changes after you have children. If you used to be comfortable with your husband being a little raunchy, maybe you can reclaim that part of yourself. If it made you uncomfortable from the beginning and you lied about it, why do you think that your husband would be any different now? Which is it? This kind of difference in sexual styles can be tremendously frustrating for both you and your husband. It may be a case where a couple should go to a therapist to mediate.

Then again, there are some special cases that can prove even more troubling:

KINKY CONNECTIONS

He wants to live out a fantasy or fetish, such as domination or spanking, that he believes his wife doesn't know about and wouldn't know how to deal with. He doesn't want to discuss it or analyze it, he just wants to do his down-and-dirty deed without complications. He goes to a prostitute because he wouldn't think of asking his wife to do it. It's uncomplicated sex with no emotional ties.

HOMOSEXUALITY

In some instances perhaps your spouse tried to be what he couldn't, and it backfired. In the situation of a mismatched sexual preference, you'll just have to deal with what is and move on, or accept the situation and make your compromises. It's difficult not to take the truth personally, but in fact it has little to do with you.

Homosexuality has a stronger place in society, and a higher level of tolerance and acceptance, than it did in the past. Antidiscrimination laws sometimes protect gays in the workplace. This was not always the case in the past, and many gay men married in order to be accepted in society and in the job market.

Some men stray, but not in the conventional way. The following story helps to illustrate a problem more common than you might think.

When I met Barry, he'd been married twenty-five years and was the father of four children. He said that he'd always been gay. That was ten years ago. He was extremely successful in business; he'd been successful in school. He loved his wife, but he was not attracted to her in the least. He was never really attracted to any woman, but he needed to be married within his career. This all sounds very trite now, but that's the way it was, so he got married; it was expected of him. It was a career move; he had to have a girl-friend, and then he had to get married. And then he had to have chil-dren and move to Connecticut.

Barry had this complete secret life. He was very much in control of his destiny in terms of business. The family was in Connecticut; it was perfectly legitimate, and he could well afford to have an apart-ment in New York because he had to stay overnight for business so often. Barry was in New York four nights a week, and he spent them with a younger lover. He was fifty-five years old and he had a quasi-monogamous relationship with a thirty-year-old guy. At this time, Barry's relationship had been going on for five years. Ron was a very handsome guy—worked out, went to law school. Barry gave Ron a job in his firm, so Ron was working for him and was paid very well.

His wife had clues but chose to ignore them. When the truth finally surfaced, it was because Barry thought his wife was having an affair, and he became jealous. He confronted her with what he thought was her infidelity. She had taken up photography and was working with young male models. He suspected her of having a sexual relationship with one of the models with whom she spent a lot of time. She told Barry that she had known of *his* escapades all along. Eventually, they reached an understanding. They agreed never to mention the other's affair and not to discuss the situation again. They stayed together because they shared so much—family and other mutual interests. The relationship actually got stronger. They didn't change; they became closer, better friends. Their sex life did not improve because Barry still found his wife unattractive. She made her own adjustments—they remained married. They needed each other. And no one ever imagined that Barry had this wild life on the side.

CHAPTER FOUR

Danger Signals:
Is Your Man a Strayer?

PAT, WIFE OF STRAYER:

You don't have to go very far to find out. Intuition is the first
clue, and then you look for the evidence to back it up. Any
change in ordinary behavior is a giveaway—like my husband
changed from twenty years of boxer shorts to bikini underwear.

❦ ❦ ❦

LET'S FACE IT, SOME MEN STRAY. We've just learned when and why it
is most likely to occur. Now we'll address the issue and be smart and
on the alert for the warning signs that indicate he may be straying—
before it's too late. The goal is to nip the problem in the bud—before
it gets out of control.

Signs can be subtle, like "the early bird special." Your husband
suddenly develops a new dedication to getting to work early—easier
to cover up than late-night dinners, and allows for long lunches! Or
there might be more obvious signs, like finding receipts for jewelry or
hotel rooms in his pants pockets . . . someone else's lingerie in the
glove compartment of his car . . . or lipstick that is not your shade on
his clothing. When you confront him, he says "You're crazy!" But you

may want to do a little detective work and see if further evidence appears. Men are often careless in covering up . . . and rarely notice the *invisible* signs, like the smell of perfume on their shirts.

To avoid getting burned, here's a simple way to tell whether your man is ready to venture outside of your relationship. A combination of any of the following may be a sign that your spouse is currently straying or about to stray:

1. Any break in the routine—he used to call you three times a day and suddenly he doesn't.
2. He starts having a lot of late-night dinner meetings.
3. His head always turns when an attractive woman walks by.
4. He's unwilling to make plans with you in advance.
5. He begins a physical shape-up program for no apparent reason.
6. He starts to pay particular attention to his clothes.
7. He buys alligator boots.
8. He comes home later and later.
9. He gives you an overly expensive gift. (Guilt is at work here.)
10. He buys a motorcycle.
11. He grows a mustache—or shaves one.
12. He talks excessively about a female coworker or any other woman.
13. He comes home regularly smelling of massage oil. (Have you met the masseuse?)
14. He's sexually distant—suddenly, he's the one with the headache; or the opposite, he overcompensates at home.
15. He's not wearing his wedding ring; he says it itches.
16. He becomes verbally abusive.
17. He starts smoking cigars.
18. You find inexplicable restaurant or hotel receipts.

19. Ditto for unrecognizable phone numbers on the bill.
20. Phone numbers written on crumpled pieces of paper fall out of his wallet or pocket.
21. He doesn't want you to accompany him on business trips.
22. He's always out with "the boys," and you're always home.
23. He gets a separate phone number and his own answering machine.
24. He trades in the family van for a sports car or equivalent symbol of his virility.
25. He goes away "by himself" on weekends.
26. His cosmetics and hair products take up more room than yours.
27. You find inexplicable seductive photos of other women left lying around.

In many cases the signs were there before you were married. Many men don't think they'll have to change their behavior once they're committed. You may have been aware of his attitude but thought things would be different after you signed the legal contract.

For example, what was his romantic background? A solo guy who's always been that way could be commitment-phobic. You might have thought he was shy or just waiting to meet the right woman— you. But what if his list of exes reads like a list of who's who in women? Some men just can't deal with monogamy.

Another critical case is the guy you married who was on the rebound. You met him when he was getting over his relationship. He needed time alone before his next connection—especially if she dumped him—but you saved him! The guy you married on the rebound could still harbor unresolved desires to get back with his ex—or to "sow wild oats" after his divorce.

Did you marry a guy who refuses to integrate into the coed world? All of his friends are still single. His idea of fun is going out with his buddies and reliving the past. He could be fifty and retelling the same old college stories and jokes and acting like a sophomoric fraternity brother. Age does not necessarily bring maturity. He didn't want to change his life, he just wanted you to fit in with his friends and be one of the guys. He's unwilling to go forward, mature, and meet new people. This is a bad sign.

Perhaps he was a noted lady's man or even a drug user. You thought you could meet the challenge and change him. The fact is, you can't change anyone but yourself. Or perhaps he was straying with you when he was married to someone else—and you thought it couldn't happen again.

You need to ask yourself if you have subconsciously recreated an unhappy pattern that you are familiar with. Listen and observe. Listening will give you the opportunity to find out exactly what you're dealing with. Don't stand by unhappily and wait for him to change. Pay attention to what he does—not what he says. What do his actions say about him?

THE COMMITMENT-PHOBIC HUSBAND

Often the signs are there from the beginning. Let me give you three instances of what happened to women who chose to marry commitment-phobic men:

Lena, twenty-five, was dating Steven, who was thirty-one years old and living at home with his extremely domineering mother. His mother said that if he married Lena, she would disown him. Lena finally persuaded Steven to marry her. He continued to live at home. She became pregnant with his child and insisted that he leave his mother. She even went to the minister who had married them. Steven moved in with Lena for a few months and then moved back in with his mother when their son was born. Lena and the baby had to move into a shelter. The baby is now three years old, and Steven is still living with his mother. Lena says she loves him and wants to be a family. She is miserable and has gained over one hundred pounds. In this bizarre situation the mother-in-law was the "other" woman.

Patti and Bob were married when they were both twenty years old. They are now twenty-seven and have two children. Patti is upset because Bob is out with the boys all the time. He wants to go to bars and watch professional sports, or go bowling and to athletic events. Bob says it's harmless and that he's just doing what he should have done when he was younger. He says he's too young to be married. They have reached an impasse. She nags him constantly to stay home. He doesn't see what her problem is.

Todd and Emma have been married for seventeen years and have five children. He is an exquisite dresser, has regular manicures, and goes to a hairstylist. He even has his eyebrows waxed. He is a restaurant manager and often has dinner with the waitresses. He likes to go to strip bars and sometimes goes on vacations without his wife. He says that she's too busy with the kids and is unattractive because she wears a warm-up suit all the time. He says he likes to have a life of his own that isn't suffocating. She has been on two talk shows trying to solve her problem.

MEN WHO ENGINEER GETTING CAUGHT

Some men leave clues for their wives to find because they secretly want to get caught. They want attention from their wives, or to provoke a crisis in their marriage. They need recognition, or they want a divorce. Some men want to torment their wives into giving them the attention they crave so they don't have to keep having affairs.

A lot of men confess to having affairs. What is their intent? Many *want* to save their marriages. Others want out.

Meet a man who got sloppy on purpose.

PHILIP, FIFTY-FIVE:

"I was married eleven years before I strayed; I was in my forties. It was a person at work and I got caught by my wife. I called the woman I was seeing and told her that I'd moved out and had an apartment. She said, 'Is this going to take long? I have a date!' What a bitch—it killed me. I did four things at the same time: I left my marriage, broke off the affair, sold my house, and changed jobs. For the first time in my life I went to a shrink. He taught me one thing—you can only control yourself! I was never in love in the first place. I got married because I moved in with this woman who had a kid and because I can't say no. She wanted to get married. I kept putting it off and then I felt guilty so I went along with it. I got caught up on the merry-go-round— doing the right things, getting the bigger car every year, the nicer house. I was playing the game. I was a meal ticket. I called the woman I was seeing from my home one night, and my wife was listening on the extension. That's how I got caught. If it hadn't been her, it would have been somebody else."

❦   ❦   ❦

HOW YOU FIND OUT

Women find out about their husbands' infidelities in a variety of ways. Some are even able to laugh about it (years later).

ELEANOR, AGE SIXTY, MARRIED THIRTY-FIVE YEARS, NOW DIVORCED, SAYS:

"One evening as I was in the kitchen making dinner, I looked out my window and saw my husband lying naked in a lounge chair in the lanai dyeing his pubic hair. I had to get close to see what he was doing. He was using the same stuff that he used for his mustache and sideburns. Then I did a little detective work and found unidentified credit-card receipts in his jacket pocket. I looked in his wallet, and there was a reservation for a local hotel. When I confronted him—and this is not a very attractive man, who is sixty-two years old—he said, 'What is it about me? Women won't leave me alone.' And the scary thing is, he was serious. He started to walk around with this 'coolness' about him. I just let him keep walking."

🌾 🌾 🌾

PAM SAYS:

"My sister-in-law's husband used to tell her he was coming home from a business trip on Friday night. He'd come home on Thursday and get a motel room with his secretary, and his wife found the receipts. I wonder why he wasn't more clever."

🌾 🌾 🌾

LINDA, AGE FORTY-FIVE, SAYS:

"My ex-husband started dyeing his hair. I noticed his hair was darker and looked dirty. He said he couldn't wash it. I was doing the laundry one day, and when I cleaned out his pockets, there were restaurant receipts from nights when he was supposed to be working late."

🌾 🌾 🌾

SHELAH, FORTY-SIX, DIVORCED LONG AGO, SAYS:

"I came home from work one night and found my husband with several other young men who looked like the Village People dancing around my bedroom, singing the song 'YMCA.' They were all wearing my jewelry, high heels, and underwear. I figured it out real fast."

☙ ☙ ☙

KIM, THIRTY-THREE, DIVORCED FROM A STRAYER, SAYS:

"I think women have intuition. You just have that feeling that something's going on. And you know what? You're always right. At first my husband said I was crazy and paranoid, but eventually he left too many clues and told too many outrageous lies."

☙ ☙ ☙

KAREN, FIFTY-TWO, IS ON HER SECOND MARRIAGE AND HAS BEEN MARRIED FOR TWENTY YEARS:

"The first time I was married, we were young and he was the love of my life. I worshiped him. I would do anything. I used to come home from work and kill myself cooking the perfect meal—perish the thought that he would stray!

"I knew immediately. No one believed me; they thought we were the perfect couple. One night he was really late and had left his wallet at home. I was concerned that he was driving without his license, so I opened his wallet to look. There was this little piece of paper folded up with a phone number on it. I called and a girl answered. Something snapped in my mind, and I knew. He came home around three in the morning and said he'd been at a card game with the guys. I told him I knew what was going on. I was the good wife, and he cheated on me.

"The next day I had a business lunch. I took my wedding ring off and left it at home. As I was leaving my office, my husband was waiting outside for me. He said he was wrong and begged me to give him another chance. I loved my in-laws and for a while I was unsure, but I knew I could never sleep with him again. He wanted to go to a marriage counselor. That night, after we went to sleep, the phone rang at two in the morning, and it was the girl on the phone. She said, 'Karen?' and all I could think was, she knows my name. I felt sick to my stomach. The next day he changed the phone number and said he'd never do it again. I told him I didn't want to go to a marriage counselor. I said, 'I'm outta here!' and took my dog and my clothes and left.

"He married the girl. She worked in his office and he had gotten her pregnant and that's what he was trying to work out. He didn't love her, but she grew on him."

❦ ❦ ❦

SAMANTHA, AGE FIFTY-THREE, SAYS:

"Let's be honest. You always think the person you marry, the person you love, your man, is going to be this knight in shining armor. I always used to say, 'Don't do that to me because it would hurt. It's humiliating and I'll go out and do it to you.' I'm talking about breaking the commitment. He did it to me, so I went out and did it to him, and guess what? He didn't like it. After twenty-eight years. That's a long time, and when that happens, you feel that a lot of your self-worth is gone. And it hurts—a lot.

"You know how I found out? I was on my boat, and I went downstairs and found my husband with my best friend. I should have thrown her overboard. He was my whole life; I met him when I was fourteen. We married when I was eighteen. In my day you went to college to find a husband. You didn't go to *be* anything. I didn't need to do that. He wouldn't have left me for her. I confronted her and she said I was imagining it. So I just left it and pushed it to the back of my mind. I threw up for three days—that gut-wrenching feeling. I've had lots of illnesses, but there is nothing as gut wrenching as when you're betrayed."

❦ ❦ ❦

KEEPING A BALANCE

The following is a story of a typical woman of her generation who did everything she was supposed to do in order to fulfill her husband's expectations of her role as wife. In doing what she thought was right, she neglected her own needs and missed out on living her life to the fullest. She gave up her personal goals and was completely absorbed by her husband's existence. He, in turn, was not challenged by the relationship and started to take her for granted. Worse, he began to look elsewhere for his excitement. Unfortunately for Pauline, she ignored the early danger signals.

PAULINE'S FRIEND SAYS:

"Pauline was married to Robert, a surgeon, for thirty-eight years; she's now going through a divorce. When she was twenty-two years old and a graduate medical technologist, she fell in love with Robert, who was a resident at the same university hospital. They married one year later and began their life together when he was finishing up his third year of residency. They moved to the suburbs and Robert settled into practice. They had four children.

"For the rest of her life, until now, Pauline was the perfect and typical physician's wife. She was a gourmet cook, an accomplished interior decorator, the president of the Junior League, the Cub Scout and Brownie leader, the PTA room mother at school, and always a devoted wife. She bought the entire program. Every single thing that was ever written up in *McCalls*, *Good Housekeeping*, or any of the other magazines' feature articles, Pauline did it, was it, lived it. One whole wall of her kitchen was cookbooks. There wasn't anything she couldn't cook or serve. There was no piece of silver or china that she didn't have.

"To go to Pauline's house for dinner was a treat. She was so warm and wonderful, and you could expect a lovely evening—until of course you went into the kitchen to help out and Robert tried to grab you in the crotch.

"About six years ago Robert stopped being as attentive. Pauline just chalked it up to his being a busy surgeon. Along with being busy all the time with his medical meetings, he started being downright mean to her. He'd insult her in public and make fun of her cooking at dinner parties. She never made a mistake, but according to Robert, everything was terrible and he'd always find something to ridicule. For instance, one day I stopped over at their house on a winter afternoon and there was the most divine aroma of raspberries throughout the house. Pauline was in the kitchen making raspberry jam. It smelled marvelous, and she was putting it in cute little gourmet bottles.

"'Gee, Robert,' I said, 'this is lovely. You don't know how lucky you are!' He said, 'You can buy Smuckers, it's better!' in front of Pauline, which was so demeaning. She didn't respond because she was the good wife.

"Then Robert had bypass surgery and said he was impotent. Pauline thought all of his behavioral changes were related to his heart problem. She tried to ignore his mood swings and the lack of sex because she was trying to be supportive and understanding. On their anniversary she begged him for any kind of affection, but he just rebuffed her. This went on for over six years. Pauline gained weight and developed psoriasis, and her personality changed—she was suddenly very introverted. You never saw her with her husband, and you used to see them everywhere. She became more and more depressed, thinking there was something wrong with her. In the last year she started to get anonymous phone calls saying, 'Your husband is having an affair.'

"One day when Pauline and I went for a walk, she told me a lot about what was going on and about Robert's impotency, and said that if she knew for sure that Robert was having an affair, the whole thing would make sense to her because it had become so awful. I gave her the names of people who would tell her the truth—people who knew her husband and worked with him. She called these people, and they told her that her husband had been having an affair with the head nurse for over six years. It was devastating, yet it was one of the most liberating things that ever happened to her, because she started to realize that she was not at fault. It was nothing she had done. Maybe the sex after thirty-seven years wasn't innovative, and she admitted that maybe she didn't do some of the more unusual things. But she said, 'If he had just shown me what he wanted, I would have done anything. But he just acted like I was ugly and horrible.' She's been in therapy for a year and has the support of almost the whole community and her four grown children. Robert lives with his mother. He still will not admit he's having an affair with the nurse, although the whole town knows it.

"The nurse is forty-seven years old and has never been married. She'd had affairs with various physicians at the hospital before she latched on to Robert. This is how she has spent her life.

"Pauline is a sixty-two-year-old woman who's about to start her life over as a single woman, and she's going to do all right. Without therapy she never would have been able to work through her anger. She says the hardest lesson she learned is that you can love somebody with your whole heart and soul, you can play by the rules and do everything right and have all the family values and the right motives, but it's a crap shoot. Because somewhere along the line, if the person you put your faith in starts operating with a whole different set of rules and doesn't tell you that the rules have changed, you're in for a shock.

"As the sex dwindled and the rotten remarks started, she should have pulled him aside. She was the dutiful wife who put up with the bull. She made excuses for him all his life—she mothered him and allowed it to happen. Because he was department chief at the hospital, none of the nurses opened their mouths. This guy was given license from his wife to behave badly and from the nurses to bully them. Basically, Pauline is a product of her generation and of the attitudes she picked up from some women's magazines."

❦   ❦   ❦

PAULINE, AGE SIXTY-TWO, MARRIED THIRTY-EIGHT YEARS, IN HER OWN WORDS:

"I had no idea how common infidelity was. There are a number of women whose husbands are professionals. They go off on trips every year, and the women know; it could be with another woman or just for a fling. One woman said to me, 'I had to make up my mind how I was going to deal with Victor. I was either going to live and fight with him constantly, or I was just going to have to accept the way he was and continue to live with it.' And that's what she's done. He's been a philanderer for years, and she knows it. I can't do that. I believe in my marriage vows. I don't believe in infidelity, and I don't want to live with a man who, every time he goes out the door, I have to wonder where he's going. I'm amazed at the men and women who came forth and supported me when I finally made the break.

"Robert has been involved with this woman on and off for fifteen years. This was a man who was home every night. She is the supervisor of nurses and has her own office. It was common for him to go there. Evidently, they would go into her office and lock the door.

"She got her job because of him. She has no management skills and can't even make a decision—Robert makes them for her. He's been doing her job for all these years.

"She's the aggressor. I was unsuspecting and naive. This was a woman who worked with my husband. If she called the house, I didn't think anything of it. We'd have parties for the nurses and she'd be there. She would come to my house at Christmastime with cookies. I treated her like a friend of Robert's.

"From the very first time I met my husband, he had this 'ideal wife' outline. She had to meet all the criteria for a doctor's wife. Granted, much of it is passé now. But she had to be good-looking, educated, she had to know how to dress and how to entertain. I bought the whole ball of wax. I tried my best in everything because this was what he wanted. He was the kind of man who, if there was a problem, he'd tell me to take care of it. So I learned to be very independent. Often I would have to take my four kids and drive eight hours to see my parents because he was working or on call.

"This woman has none of that. She's not good-looking and she doesn't know how to dress; people ridicule her. She shaves her eyebrows and paints on fake ones. She wears too much obvious makeup and her hair always looks awful. She has no shape at all. She has gone from one affair with a married man to another. She's forty-seven and he's sixty-three. She was involved with my husband's competition before him. She thinks she and my husband will be married. My friends think he will marry her to justify his actions.

"Let me tell you how I found out about the affair. First of all, he was becoming more and more abusive to me. Not physically, but mentally and verbally. For five years my daughters told me to leave him because he was so abusive. I begged him to go into therapy or counseling. He wouldn't go, but I did. That helped me to hang on for a while. It was getting worse and worse. One day there was a message on my answering machine: 'Do you know your husband's having an affair?' I saved the message and let him listen to it. He said that people are always making those remarks about doctors. It happened a few more times.

"On the night of our thirty-seventh anniversary we had dinner with some very old friends of ours. Robert was absolutely obnoxious at dinner and got staggering drunk. When we left the restaurant, our friends told him he couldn't drive home. We had an argument and he took the keys from me. He was abusive the whole way home, saying he could drive drunk better than I could drive sober. He dropped me off and said he was going to sleep in the office. I couldn't sleep; it was our anniversary and I was worried about him. I drove to his office to make sure he was okay. He wasn't there and his car was not in the parking lot. That's when I knew he had to be with someone. He didn't come home until the following morning. The next day my daughter and I went to a lawyer's office.

"I was suspicious but I didn't know for sure. What was his pattern? He was never out at night; we had a social life, we entertained, we went on vacations together and to family gatherings.

That to me is a marriage. Our sex life had become nil, but he has a heart condition and had open-heart surgery, and that is a side effect. He was impotent; he couldn't function. I am convinced that he just couldn't perform with me. When he first had a heart attack, he got drunk one night. We came home and he wanted sex but he couldn't perform and blamed me. He was drunk; that's why he couldn't do it. From then on there were times he could perform and times he could not. We had sex maybe once every two months, and only if I initiated it. I felt sorry for him. Sex is very important to Robert. I realize now how important. If I initiated it and he couldn't perform, he felt bad and I felt bad, and it just made matters worse. So I didn't pursue it. I allowed us to drift apart, and he, being involved, let it happen. I thought he didn't initiate sex with me because he wasn't functional. Maybe I was in denial. I kept making excuses for him.

"I thought a lot of his verbal abuse was his taking it out on me because of what he was having to deal with. I became more and more independent—he took that to mean that I didn't need him or his money, which bothered him. I don't know that I could have done anything differently. I couldn't communicate with him. He's never wrong, and he never takes the blame for anything; it always gets passed on to someone else. This is part of his personality. I was constantly making excuses for him.

"This was not his first affair. I have recently learned that there were several before the head nurse. There was a girl who used to work in his office, and I was convinced they had had an affair. I confronted him and he said that I was just jealous of her. Then there was another girl my son's age. They used to stop taking patients at three-thirty and go in the office and close the door.

"It's a year of therapy later, so I can talk about it now. I was a crazy woman a year ago. I keep asking my friends what I could have done. They tell me I was too busy doing my job being the perfect wife, the perfect mother, the perfect hostess, and the perfect community volunteer. I had a business and a full life. He goes out and picks this slut.

"Sometimes I wonder if she knows the pain and suffering she has caused my family. My four children won't talk to their father. He says the divorce is 'just between your mother and me.' He's living with his eighty-eight-year-old mother who won't talk to me, and we'd been very close for almost forty years. I worry about my children's inheritance. If he marries her, she will get the money that my children are entitled to.

"I'll tell you what keeps me together: a wonderful circle of friends, four great kids, and a good therapist. You know, I still love him, but I hate him for what he's done to our family."

🌿 🌿 🌿

This is a sad story, but much can be learned from it. Not the least of this is the fact that Pauline said that she wonders if the woman was aware of the pain she had caused. This is yet another case of the dangers posed by "availability," and of women's inhumanity to women. This woman went ahead with a long-term affair, fully aware that the man was married, even going to the house that he shared with his wife.

The last six years were so traumatic for Pauline that she was beaten down when she finally left. Had she given her husband an ultimatum to see a counselor when she had first been aware of the problem, she could have saved herself a lot of heartache. Fortunately, Pauline finally had the strength to leave. She sought professional help and was able to get on with her life.

HOW TO PROTECT YOURSELF

It may be that you are not prepared to change because you have not evaluated the situation. You must ask yourself, "What am I getting out of this experience? If I were to make this decision, would it help me grow? Would it bring me more happiness? If I stay the way I am, what will happen? Am I resisting change because I am afraid or too comfortable?" In the end, the right decision is spiritually inspired by the inner self.

                                 ↝ NANA VEARY

Are you ready to feel your way and find your own rules? You have to have self-respect and know if it's time to move on and save your own life. You're going to focus on the things that will make a difference in *your* life, and you're going to stay focused in order to achieve your goals. This is an opportunity to develop new and winning patterns. You can decide to eliminate the negatives that drove him away—or you can decide that it's time for a new beginning!

Your response should be as well planned and thought out as a businessperson's strategic plan. You can develop a strategy for saving your marriage—or leaving it, depending on what you decide is best for *you*. Like any business plan, you should choose your strategy, set time limits, and review your progress as you move ahead. Remember, in any business deal desperation shows. You have to be willing to make your best offer and give it your best shot.

This will take work—and courage. Neediness and desperation are big turn-offs, but in the back of your mind you must feel and sincerely know that your happiness does not depend on keeping the strayer in your life. If your plan doesn't work, it's not the end of the world. With that in mind you can proceed with confidence and a positive attitude and know you have given it your best, committed effort. Remember that you are in this for *you.*

I want to tell you a story that a multimillionaire businessman told me recently that helped me understand just how powerful knowing what you want can be. I had the opportunity to use his tactic, and to my surprise it worked. I think you will agree that it relates directly to how we act in relationships.

Jerry, a successful businessman, saw a vacation house that he liked, which was offered at $2 million. On the day he saw the house, he made an offer of $1 million in cash with a thirty-day close. This was a clean deal with no banks involved. The real-estate broker said she wouldn't insult the owner with the offer.

A few months later another person attempted to purchase the house for close to the asking price, but the deal fell through. The broker called Jerry and asked if he was still interested. He said yes, at the same offer of $1 million. The broker tried to negotiate. Jerry calmly stated that his offer was non-negotiable. Subsequently, another deal came around on the house. By this time the owners were desperate to sell, as their family was expanding and they did not have enough room. The second deal fell through, and once again the broker contacted Jerry. He said his offer was the same. The owner and the broker tried to move him up a few hundred thousand. Jerry wouldn't budge. Then the owner said that some of the items that were supposed to be included at $2 million were not part of the deal. Jerry said, "No deal!" Eventually, he got the house for $1 million dollars, and on his terms. I asked him if he didn't feel bad that the seller had to take half of his asking price. "Not at all," Jerry said. "No one forced him to take the deal."

Jerry said he loved the house and had wanted it from the moment he'd looked at it. I said, "You could have afforded to go up in price. Weren't you afraid of losing the house?" He answered that in business you can't ever really want or need anything *that* badly. Another house would have come along. You decide what something is worth to you, and it has nothing to do with what the other person paid for it, says it's worth, or wants for it. It has to do with you and what you are willing to do to get it. "Desperation always shows," he said. "Emotionally detach yourself for the moment and be smart."

I thought he was probably right, and that the same was true for relationships. And then I thought of what my grandmother used to say: "Never chase after a bus or a man. Another one will come along in about two minutes."

CHAPTER FIVE

How to Recognize a Strayer

Sometimes I wonder if men and women really suit each other. Perhaps they should live next door and just visit now and then.

☞ KATHARINE HEPBURN

DAVE, RESTAURANT MANAGER, DIVORCED:

"Q: Do you equate marriage with monogamy?

A: Only if they're both in town at the same time!"

FAMOUS STRAYERS IN HISTORY

Don Juan
Casanova
John F. Kennedy
Reverend Dimmesdale
    (with Hester Prynne)
Jimmy Carter (but only in his heart)
FDR

Henry VIII (although he married
    them all)
Charlie Chaplin
Lord Byron
Anthony Quinn
Prince Charles

How to Recognize a Strayer

There are many different kinds of strayers—with different backgrounds, various causes for their straying, and a whole spectrum of different behaviors. However, keeping in mind that there are exceptions to every rule, it is possible to make some generalizations about their common traits:

	The Strayer	*The Stayer*
The Connection	He hasn't quite made the transition into married life. He still thinks of himself as single and hangs around with his single friends, going to sports events or out for a beer with the guys. He often looks at other women.	He's in this for the long haul and is totally committed. Friends and family members overlap with those of his spouse. They integrate into each other's lives.
Let's Talk	The strayer's favorite words are still, "I" and "My." "*I* want to go here." "It's *my* money."	He thinks of himself and his wife as partners, and he talks that way. He uses words like "we" and "our" and discusses issues with his wife. He's interested in getting her input before making major decisions that affect both of them. He's more likely to say, "Let's do this," than "I want to." He's a team player.
Wardrobe	He wears more jewelry and spends more money than you on manicures and hair styling. He subscribes to GQ and needs more closet space than you. He may have his ear pierced and wear a stud earring.	He usually dresses neatly, casually, and fairly conservatively. He's not overly concerned with his appearance. You won't find him at your hairdresser or manicurist. He may even go to the local barber. You probably buy his clothes for him.

	The Strayer	*The Stayer*
Vacations	He goes by himself (or so he says).	This guy might take his kids camping to give his wife a weekend off, or take his whole family to Disney World. Better yet, he and his wife sneak away for a romantic rendezvous. When he goes to his high-school or college reunion, he takes his wife.
Careers	He's likely to be in one of the following professions: Sports figure Actor Musician Surgeon Traveling salesman	He's a family man and likes to be with his wife and kids. He's probably a: Accountant Psychologist Computer programmer Construction worker Small business owner Teacher
Entertainment	The strayer's heroes and role models may include known womanizers. He devours books like Anthony Quinn's autobiography *One Man Tango* which romanticizes the fact that he had twelve children by two wives and three mistresses. He still loves to watch James Bond movies. He reads *Playboy* and the Victoria's Secret catalog.	Every year he renews his subscription to *Sports Illustrated*. He goes to the movies with his family. His favorite books include *The Cat in the Hat* and anything by Michael Crichton.

Strayers come in all types, and some are more easily recognizable than others. Many of us came across them when we were single—and some of us are married to them. Some are only temporarily "lost" and can be turned around. Others stray through no fault of yours, and you are best off without them. If you discover you are married to a permanently commitment-phobic man, be smart and do the positive thing: move on. Don't waste any more time.

MEET THE STRAY CATS

JAMES, FIFTY-FIVE:

"Ninety-five percent of the married men who have been married over thirty years have strayed. My has brother fantasized about having affairs, but he's never cheated. Now he's so jealous of people who have. He loves his wife, but he feels he's missing out on something."

🌿 🌿 🌿

What follows is a series of brief profiles of temporary strayers. These strayers can sometimes be reformed—although only you can decide if it's worth the effort. Although they display a multitude of behaviors, the summaries will give you a good idea of the kinds of men to watch out for. Have you ever met any of these?

The "Special K" Stray

He can't resist his nurse, personal trainer, or massage therapist. He's addicted to the *professional* attention. Remember the old saying, "An idle mind is the devil's workshop"—keep him busy at home, and you won't have to worry about his tendency to roam.

"I'm Okay, You're Okay" Stray

He's a professional man, possibly a physician or attorney. He tends to take advantage of his relationships with weak or vulnerable women—he might even be their therapist. (Talk about mind-fuckers!)

Fear-of-Gray Stray

These strayers are suffering through your basic midlife crisis. He thinks an affair will help him regain his youth—and possibly his hair. Most men eventually grow out of this phase. In your case, perhaps this too shall pass.

Far-and-Away Stray

This is a common result of a long-distance marriage. Typically, he's on the road more than he is at home. He has his own agenda when he's traveling. It may start out innocently enough, just someone to have dinner with, and end up a full-blown affair. He will stray when he's away.

Have-a-Nice-Day Stray

He can't resist the checkout girl. She's the person he sees every day—the casual, ditsy person behind the counter where he buys his coffee or newspaper, or the girl at the checkout counter at a mall store. He finds he has to acknowledge her presence—beyond putting the money on the counter.

Pay-for-Play Stray

He's willing to remunerate. It's pretty cut-and-dried. If it's a prostitute, he's in it for momentary sexual gratification, not a relationship. Hollywood madam Heidi Fleiss made a lot of money off these guys. These men rationalize that they pay for a date one way or the other. In the more accepted form, they hope to get sex after an expensive date. With a prostitute, they reason, at least it's "honest." It's also uncomplicated, with no emotional ties. This kind of stray could also involve a long-term mistress. It's a double life for a guy who pays the rent, sends a monthly check, and might even put her in his will!

Romp-in-the-Hay Stray

This guy is a snake charmer. He goes from woman to woman, falling in and out of love. This kind of stray fits our traditional conception of the model strayer; he is charming and probably looks the part and brags about it.

The Rainy-Day Stray

He's addicted to the one-night stand. Often it's with a complete stranger he meets on the plane or in a cab, or someone he meets on a business trip. It's an isolated moment and no one will ever know. The danger and excitement are the attraction.

The Fey Stray

He's committed to fantasy; maybe he's hooked on the illusion of *Penthouse* pets or videos. He's harmless—he just needs more attention. Something has changed in the relationship, and he is feeling insecure. It could be the birth of a baby, or a wife's new job, causing a shift of focus from him to the kids, job, or other activities. Perhaps his wife has lost the zest for sex that she once had. He doesn't want an affair, so he escapes into fantasies with girlie magazines—or even at strip bars.

The Power-Play Stray

He's attracted to the young *babe*; he's always older than she is. She's attracted to him because he has the money and the toys. He's had more time to acquire things. It's easy for the power stray to knock the nerdy boyfriend out of competition. The boyfriend's not as attractive, has no money, and lives a mundane life. The young woman becomes the power stray's trophy. Her youth and beauty are her power. He now has greater stature. Power is an aphrodisiac to many women—they throw themselves at men in positions of power, who are usually very wealthy.

"It's Not the Same Way" Stray

He wants to check out a woman he finds exotic, someone of another race or culture. He may have a fetish—like a foot or a leg fetish, or a desire to find out if redheads have red pubic hair.

Spousal-Okay Stray

Hard to believe? *I* thought so; then I spoke with some women involved. One woman said she'd rather know whom her husband's going to be with than have him "knocking all about," so she just puts up with it. He's had a relationship with the "other woman" for fifteen years. And she's not who you would think of as the threatening "other woman." She's a very attractive, charming, and well-educated woman of the same age as the strayer's wife.

The "Hey" Stray

This is the talking, or mental, stray. The couple is attracted to each other, and they build up each other's ego through attention and conversation. They wouldn't ruin it by consummation. Brendan, thirty-two, says, "One time I went to bed with a talking affair, and it was the most disappointing thing ever."

The "Eye" Stray

Then there are the more exotic variants on straying. For example, Sela, age fifty-three, who has been married thirty-two years, reports on one specialized type:

"I call it eye-fucking; it's where he does it with eye contact. I see my husband doing this so often. It infuriates me, and I've told him a few times in no uncertain terms. It happens most frequently at airports. Recently, my husband and I were on a plane and could not be seated together. I walked up the aisle to tell him something before we landed, and I saw him doing it with this woman across the aisle. I turned and walked away, but I told him later, 'The next time you do that in my company, I'm not going to just tell you off, I'm going to tell her.' I'll probably tell her that he does this all the time, and 'Don't think you're going to get a wedding ring on your finger, honey. It's just his game.'

"On our most recent flight we get on the plane, and because he's been screwing around so much and being so vain, we are the last people on. We're in our seats way in the back. He was doing the eye thing with this very attractive woman. She walked by him on the way to the ladies' room and returned the look. He took his *USA Today* and held it over the aisle. When he hears the toilet door open, he drops the middle of the paper so he can pick it up and do the eye thing, and the biggest, fattest man walked by. It was the wrong toilet. I looked at him and said, 'Well, that one didn't work.'"

Permanent Strayers

In most cases the permanent strayer cannot be redeemed. He's probably gone for good, but you can learn from the experience.

On-the-Way Stray

For much of his married life this man went through the motions of living happily. Typically, he has recently recovered from a life-threatening illness or accident in which he almost died. He leaves for another woman—usually younger. Unfortunately for the wife, this guy wants to make the most of his final years in a new "second life."

He sees it as his last chance. He wants to live life to the fullest. You're out, she's in. Wish him well and let him go in peace.

The Gay Stray

How can you compete? In these cases it's better just to let nature take its course and move on to someone with the same orientation as you.

The Cultural Stray

It's in his genes. In some cultures infidelity isn't as big an issue as it is in ours. It's a way of life for him, and he sees nothing wrong with it. If you grew up in the same culture, you may find the situation tolerable, but if not, you'll never be happy with his attitudes about marriage, relationships, or commitment. Keep in mind that it's unlikely he will change his behavior. For example, actress and politician Melina Mercouri has said, "The average Greek man is a good friend and a good husband—although he has infidelity in his blood."

May-Day Stray

He's not in love anymore and he wants out—now. The love that made him commit is somehow gone and he's sure it can't be rekindled. Perhaps his reasons for committing in the first place were not real. He might have been too young. For these men straying is about making changes in their lives. It's unlikely that he'll change his mind.

Every-Which-Way Stray

Many men lead a dual existence. In this case a temporary affair is prolonged into an ongoing one that can endure for many years. He may say he can't leave his wife because she is dying or it will break him financially to get a divorce. He spends holidays with his wife, but most of the time he is truly "absent."

In many cases he's gotten away with his double life for so long, he doesn't think there's anything wrong with it. His wife may pretend she doesn't know, and his girlfriend pretend she doesn't care. He gets the best of both worlds—the caring, nurturing, and companionship of two women.

The Animal Stray

He still loves his wife, but he cannot curb his lust for other women. The serial adulterer goes from woman to woman. He's not totally committed in his primary relationship. He doesn't stay around his home to provide support for his wife and family. This guy is a PIG. His ego and entire sense of self continue to lie in how many women he can have. He believes that he was meant to be a "hunter and gatherer." His strongest drive is to pursue women—as many as possible.

With the prevalence of AIDS, this could be dangerous. You may also spend too much valuable time wondering and worrying that he will turn into a permanent strayer. More than likely, the danger signals were all there from the beginning. Did you know ahead of time? Perhaps you expected him to change. This kind never does.

The following scenario is possibly one of the most difficult situations to assess and respond to. He often says he loves his wife and that he's happy. In reality he's just a pig—and you have to decide how to deal with him.

THE MOST DANGEROUS STRAYER

JAKE, AGE THIRTY-NINE, MARRIED NINE YEARS, SAYS:

"I do not equate marriage with monogamy. Yes, I stray, but it's not once a week. It's occasionally—I would say nine times since I've been married. When my wife met me, I was dating three other women. My wife and I lived together for three years before being married. When we were living together, I still saw other women. I was married under six months when I first strayed. If my wife ever found out, it would crush her, and rightly so. She has been betrayed, but I guess I never considered that. I say if it's done properly in this day and age, it's okay. With AIDS it's trickier. Some care certainly has to be taken.

"You see, it's not that I don't love my wife. I love my wife dearly. I strayed because of interest. Maybe it's curiosity rather than interest. I've always loved women, and so if the opportunity presented itself and I felt it was something that could be done without their turning around and falling in love with me, I would pursue it. I have always made a point of saying, 'Hey, I can have an affair, but you know what my situation is. You know I'm not going to leave my wife.' It has always been more of a sexual thing than heartfelt love.

"I love her to death. She's good in bed, she takes good care of me as far as my needs in the home and everything like that. She thinks a lot like I do as far as we don't intend to have children. If she ever found out and felt she wanted to leave, I would be deeply hurt. If she threatened to leave, I believe I could stop. It's not like I'm a sex junkie.

"I'm looking for sex and adventure. I'm definitely not looking for a relationship. I find a lot of women are intrigued by the possibility, maybe because the scenario is 'You're getting away with something.' But maybe I bring out a certain thing in these women as far as I'm giving them something they need in terms of support. Some of my best friends have been women, which I'm sure is related to how I run into women. I've always been what I consider to be a good listener. I don't know what the attraction is. Like I say, it's not a targeted thing, it's more of a feeling you get when you're talking to somebody. You say, 'Hey, I'd like to have a glass of wine with you,' and that type of thing.

"I've been with married women, widows, women ten years my junior—quite an array, even ex-girlfriends. It's not a specific type. I meet them through the workplace. I've worked for them, they've worked for me. I'm not a bar goer; I don't go out looking, or anything of that nature. It's more of a casual crossing, I guess. I'm accused of not having morals, but that's not true. In business I'm very moral.

"I work for a lot of women, so if they call me at home, I have an excuse. Some women know my wife, and they're amazed that my wife doesn't realize that we've been together. I tell them that some people are in love to the point of stupidity, and some people, as in my wife's case, trust me to the point where she doesn't even consider it.

"I've never gone out looking for an affair. I casually say something to someone, and if the reaction is something that makes me think they're interested too, then I pursue it. But I'd never make the effort to get them to change their mind. The spontaneity is very exciting, which, of course, it is in any relationship. It's not like I wake up in the morning and say, 'Today I'm going to go find a blond!' That's not the whole point of it. But when you find something that's spontaneous, that in itself is arousing. Some people couldn't do it because they'd feel too terrible the next day. I can't say I do.

"My strays lasted anywhere from one night to two and a half years. I don't get attached. It's always been a mutual thing, ending it or starting it. The married women I strayed with were happy. They were just looking for . . . more or less adventure, something different. There's a certain amount of thrill as far as getting away with it. I guess you could say that the women I've been with cared more for me than I for them. No matter how honest I've been, I still think that to some extent there's a hurt. Although I've never been hurt by the situation.

"I wear a wedding ring. It's out in the open; I'm married, I love my wife. When I have sex, no women have requested that I take it off. They mainly ask me to take off my pants. I've never had a woman say, 'I can't do it when you're wearing that ring.'

"The sex is always different. Some isn't so good, and on occasion some is better. But I think that has to do with the individual's sexuality, because sex is only what you make it. If both parties enjoy it and are uninhibited, I think you have a tendency to have better sex. I don't think that love is necessarily a part of sex.

"If my wife was having an affair, I'd say 'Are you lacking something from me, or is this just a fling?' I enjoy my home and I enjoy spending time with my wife. I consider myself to be a good husband. I'm caring and affectionate, maybe overly so. When my wife's sick, I take good care of her. If she goes out with the girls, I don't give her the third degree. I'm not a possessive type of person. Possession just chokes the relationship.

"As far as what women can do to keep their man from straying—quite truthfully, they should be less inhibited sexually. I don't know if I have these affairs because my wife is slightly inhibited or if it's just because the other women offer something different. If my wife was any kinkier, I don't know if it would change things. I would still be attracted to other women."

🌾 🌾 🌾

Men like this are hard to deal with because they leave no clue—they have no guilt. The "nice guy" who comes home every night and acts like the perfect husband is more difficult to recognize as a strayer or potential strayer. Are there any other aspects in his behavior that would give him away?

CLIFF, AGE FIFTY, WORKING ON HIS SECOND MARRIAGE, SAYS ABOUT STRAYING:

"Personally, I don't think I know one guy in my life, except maybe my father—and I don't really know about him—who didn't stray at one time. The bottom line is it's going to happen, and it should be everybody's understanding when they get married that the man is not going to be faithful. Everybody strays! Everybody! If you're twenty-two years old or thirty years old and you think your marriage means fidelity, you're wrong. If you think a guy can stay married for forty or fifty years and not jump on someone else, you're wrong. It's going to happen—it's how you deal with it that matters. Marriage isn't just based on sex, but if it's bad sex or no sex, then you probably have a permanent stray. But the fact is, the traditional vision of a monogamous marriage will never work—it's impossible. It's been going on for thousands of years. I do not equate marriage with monogamy.

"Marriage can work, but it's not going to work based on fidelity. One of the biggest-selling books of all time is *The Bridges of Madison County* because it hit a chord. All that book is about is dissatisfaction and unhappiness; that is the key to everything. The woman was dissatisfied. Men stray when they are dissatisfied. Why do they stay? Fear of financial insecurity. Most people can't support two households. Fear of the unknown—the devil you know is better than the devil you don't."

🌿 🌿 🌿

Marrying a man is like buying something you've been admiring for a long time in a shop window. You may love it when you get it home, but it doesn't always go with everything else.

☞ JEAN KERR

I've met men over the years whom I know to be married, yet they come across as single and totally available. It's as though they have never really made the transition into a committed marital partnership. They talk as if they're single. Sometimes they are so overtly flirtatious that it's hard to believe they're married. In other cases the husband and wife lead very separate lives and are rarely in the same place at the same time. This can work if they are both happy with the situation. More often, however, at least one party—you?—is extremely unhappy.

CHAPTER SIX

Women Men Stray With

BERT, FIFTY-SEVEN:

"What kind of women do men stray with? Anyone who winks
back, but doesn't suffer from blepharitis!"

🌿 🌿 🌿

THE "OTHER WOMAN" IS NOT ALWAYS AS OBVIOUS as Hester Prynne
displaying a scarlet *A* on her chest. And she may not fit your conception of the model strayee. She could be your best friend, in
whom you have confided your most intimate marital secrets. The
other woman could have started as a casual, opposite-sex friend of
your husband. She might be the woman sitting next to him on the
plane or even his ex-wife, whom he's been saying the most awful
things about.

THE WOMEN MEN STRAY WITH CAN BE:

Coworkers

Their secretaries

Their wife's close friend

Any woman who spells Jennifer
    with a G instead of a J

Women who love frequent sex

Younger women

Flight attendants

Waitresses

Masseuses

Married women (who are not
    looking for a commitment)

Women who don't expect too
    much

Prostitutes (for instant gratification
    without commitment)

His ex-wife (the poison you know is
    better than the one you don't)

Someone who shares a strong
    mutual interest

Today's talk shows are filled with guests accusing their best friends of deliberately stealing their husbands—the supreme betrayal. I have had similar brushes with disloyalty. One night, when my best friend in high school and I were double-dating, I asked my boyfriend if he'd mind dropping her off on his way home. They never quite made it home, and needless to say, I was devastated when I found out they had spent the night necking. I felt more betrayed by my female friendship than I ever could have by any summer romance.

I have to admit, I'm no saint. Some years ago when I was long divorced, my friend's ex-husband asked me out. I thought it over (for about ten seconds) and managed to convince myself that they were through, he was up for grabs, and she wasn't that close a friend anyway. I dated him quietly for several months, but I considered this to be only a mild betrayal. It's not as if I did something mean—I was just rationalizing and looking out for myself. Nevertheless, she would have been furious if she'd ever found out, and I never told her.

Mia Farrow was a good friend and frequent houseguest of André and Dori Previn in the late sixties. Mia later ran off and married André, leaving Dori Previn to write and sing sad songs about her loss and betrayal. Years later Mia Farrow had to deal with the ultimate betrayal when her adopted daughter Soon-Yi moved in with her lover, Woody Allen. Who said what goes around comes around?

MEN STRAY WITH WOMEN WHO ARE:	
Younger	Have similar thoughts and interests
Affectionate	Are unhappily married to someone
Attentive	else
Sexy	

Ethics don't seem to get in the way much when a woman wants a man. So be on the lookout. Men will always stray because the availability of women to stray with is never in short supply. There is not a *typical* strayee; the only constant is availability.

WHERE THE GIRLS ARE

Women in certain situations are more likely to stray. She might be the confidante of the man in a business relationship. As his personal assistant, the woman often knows more about her boss and his whereabouts than his own wife does. He knows her and relies on and trusts her. When things go wrong at home, she is the first person he turns to. They have a business relationship without any of the aggravations at home. He sees her at her best, and she generally dotes on him. She is the subordinate, and he has power over her; his wish is her command.

The Workplace

The workplace has changed significantly and has become a breeding ground for straying. Now there's a whole sector of available females who share interests with other women's husbands. Whereas years ago the only women workers were secretaries over sixty, or twenty-year-old girls looking for husbands, this has not been the case for some time. Female coworkers share interests similar to your husband's, and your husband is with them all day. They go on business trips together, and it's a situation that's easy to hide. Men say that work is primarily the place where they do their straying.

PETER, THIRTY-FOUR, SAYS:

"Propinquity, space, and common thoughts and interests are very powerful. Essentially what happens, and I've seen it over and over, is that you have a husband who is tied up in work and a wife who basically has no interest in his work whatsoever, and suddenly he finds himself with somebody else who shares all of his interests, and he's with that person all the time.

"If I told my wife that I'd slept with my secretary, she could probably live with that. She understands what it is for a younger woman to use her body to get something she wants. But if I came home and said that I met this woman at work, and we've taken long walks on the beach, and we talk about religion and life, and I really love her—it would hurt her much more than 'I screwed my secretary.'"

🌿 🌿 🌿

Available women are everywhere. Men meet them at the following places:

The Supermarket

GEORGE, FORTY-SEVEN:

"If I want to meet women, I go to the supermarket. I see more attractive women with a completely bored, vacant look on their faces. In Vietnam we used to call it 'the thousand-yard stare.'"

🌿 🌿 🌿

Alcoholics Anonymous

WALTER:

"I fell in love with Anne but I didn't consummate it. I could never leave my family. Anne understood me, and we had so much in common. It was mental infidelity. I still love her!"

🌿 🌿 🌿

Sports Activities

If you don't go to the game with him, he may find someone else who will share his enthusiasm.

Your Home

How often do we hear of the husband running off with his wife's best friend who used to visit? Or how about the baby-sitter? Robin Williams married the woman who cared for his kids during his first marriage.

Church

He may think it's a religious experience.

THE WOMEN

As you will see from reading the following stories, the kinds of women men stray with may come as a big shock. They are not the trampy, hated, stereotypical "other woman." It could be a very close friend or someone you least suspect—a woman he is comfortable with and who pays attention to him. Bob, divorced and forty-two years old, said it succinctly: "I wasn't looking for a young girlfriend. I was looking for an old wife who knows all my friends!"

Meg has been a strayee since she was nineteen years old, when she had her first affair with one of her married college professors. The affair lasted ten years, and now they are "just friends." I found her to be precocious and funny, but not a classic beauty. In the first fifteen minutes of meeting me, she made her uninhibited sexuality apparent. She told me she had bought a pair of black patent-leather five-inch spike heels. When I looked surprised and asked how she could walk in them, she laughed and answered, "I wear them with the heels pointing at the ceiling."

Meg explained that her intimate relationships have all been with married men. Her only other male friend is gay. She claims that married men are the only men she meets who ask her out.

Married men pursue her for sexual gratification, then drop her. She dresses up for them and is sexually uninhibited. This, they confide to her, is something their wives will not do. It is unlikely that any of them would seriously consider leaving their spouses for Meg. Rather, she is a toy to play with. She does, however, possess that uninhibited sexuality that many men are looking for when they are bored or unhappy at home. As for Meg, she obviously experiences a fear of intimacy, so she surrounds herself with unavailable men.

LEROY, MARRIED TWENTY-SIX YEARS, SAYS:

"Something that has always fascinated me is that I've known a number of people who have left their wives for someone else, and from an objective standpoint, the one they're leaving their spouse for is not as attractive."

❦ ❦ ❦

Men need constant ego reinforcement and women need love reinforcement. Men stray with women who will boost their egos. They are more likely to stray with someone way below their stature, who is not a threat. The wife might be a well-educated society woman who has raised their children.

THOMAS, THIRTY-FIVE, SAYS:

"I think that when a man strays or has a dalliance, it's with somebody very different from his wife. There's a secretary at my office who is what we all call 'exquisitely cheap.' She chews gum and wears skirts that are way too short and dresses that are much too sexy for the office. Her hair is very teased, and she wears too much makeup and push-up bras. But she has an incredibly beautiful body, and she's really attractive and very sexy in a cheap way. She is very nice, but she really is exquisitely cheap. You want her, but you wouldn't want to marry her or bring her to the investment-banking picnic or an important business dinner. But you could easily imagine yourself taking a long lunch hour if a friend of yours had an apartment within walking distance of the office. That's one kind of woman men stray with."

❦ ❦ ❦

DUKE, A FORTY-FOUR-YEAR-OLD STRAYER, SAYS:

"Men stray with women who have characteristics that are different or opposite from their wives—for example, somebody who's extremely smart in your business and who understands everything you're doing and going through at work and how complex it is. And, of course, we all think that our work is terribly complex and very few people can understand the intricacy of what we do. But here's a woman that does; she doesn't necessarily have to be attractive, but she understands you and what you do, and she's attracted to you and tells you, and it's flattering because somebody likes you for your brain, and you like her for her brain. Mostly, it's your coworker."

❦ ❦ ❦

FELICE, HAPPILY MARRIED FOR MOST OF
THIRTY-FOUR YEARS, SAYS:

"What can you do to make a man not stray? There isn't anything you can do because there are no guarantees that he is not having a fling on the side. Women like other women more than men like men. However, that doesn't mean your best friend isn't going after your husband. It happens more often than not because that's who it usually is. It's the secretary, the nurse, or the best friend, because that's who they meet, and that's who they have a history with. A man will not leave his wife for someone he meets in a bar. A bar is a one-night stand, but a relationship or an affair is a best friend or a coworker."

❦ ❦ ❦

Women are more independent and predatory than they used to be and have higher expectations of men. When I started to write this book, I was not aware of how aggressive women can be when they want a certain man. There are hundreds of women out there who are going to make your man feel good just by showering him with attention and flattery. There are no killer issues like money or children to get in the way. These "play strays" are there for fun, and they don't care about you or your family or your future.

Recently, I was at a party with my husband. I met a friend who cornered me on the way in the door, so it appeared for a short time that my husband was alone as he entered the room. Two women approached him and were very flirtatious. I watched in stunned silence and then excused myself and walked over to join him. One woman returned to her escort. The other insisted on continuing a dialogue. "Bill and I were just trying to figure out how we knew each other," she said to me. "Really!" I smiled through gritted teeth and then introduced myself as Bill's wife. This did nothing to dissuade her.

Women tend to size each other up. She was wearing fishnet stockings and a lace minidress. She had to be in her late forties. Her hair was an unattractive blond with black roots. She was a close talker. She sauntered around my husband and touched his arm as she talked. As I steered him to our table, I said, "I can't believe how bold that woman is," and then more emphatically added, "What a cheesy, predatory broad!"

"See?" he said. "You have just proven my theory that women don't like other women. Look what you just called that woman you don't even know." The other woman (a massage therapist), who was seated at another table with her boyfriend, came over to our table and asked if she could borrow my husband's jacket, which was hanging on the back of his chair. She said she was cold. My husband thought my appalled reaction was hilarious. "You see," he said, "I'm a fifty-year-old guy who is balding, and look what happens. Imagine if John Kennedy, Jr., came into this room. We're not talking about all men looking like Robert Redford. The average guy goes out and has a few drinks and anybody starts to look good at midnight. And she's there, it's just so available. The point is, they're there. That's what your book should be about, the availability of women and their lack of scruples, because that's the reason men stray."

WHY WOMEN "STRAY"

Many women who never intended to stray are surprised to see how quickly their life can change—and how easy it is to become the "other woman" a man strays with.

DIANE SAYS:

"I was twenty-two years old when I met Noel. He was thirty-three and married to my roommate's sister, Julia. One night my roommate invited me to her sister and her husband's country club. I had met Julia on a couple of occasions but had never met her husband.

"So we went to this country club, and the next day Julia called and said that her husband thought I was absolutely terrific and that if he weren't married, he would want to be married to me. At twenty-two, looking at this old man of thirty-three, I was turned off. I had no attraction to him at all.

"Over the years, no matter where I would go, Noel would find somebody who knew me to send his regards. He was crazy about me. Every summer I would go to Europe. I was a teacher during the day and a waitress at night. He found out where I was working, and one night he came to have dinner—alone. Again, I had no interest in him. I found it funny and cute. I wasn't at a stage in my life even to be thinking in those terms. You have to be pretty lonely to get involved with a married man. I wasn't lonely at the time, but he pursued me.

"My former roommate got engaged and asked me to be the maid of honor, and Noel's wife was the matron of honor. I brought a date. I did not want to be near Noel. There was nothing about him that I liked. He was blond—I always went for dark-haired men. He kept trying to ask me to dance, and my date kept cutting in, like I told him to.

"I moved in with this guy I was seeing. We lived together for three years until one day he came home and told me he was leaving me, and that he'd been screwing around with the wife of this couple that we used to double-date with all the time. When he left me, I was devastated. I was in love with him, and I thought we would get married.

"That's when my former roommate called me. She was very happily married with a baby. She told me that her sister, Julia, had just moved and lived right near me and that I should go see her. It would make me feel better. I don't know why I did it, but I called her up and said I just heard she moved into the neighborhood and I'd like to come over and say hello. When I got there, Noel wasn't there—he was out playing golf—but he called to say what time he'd be home. His wife said, 'You're never going to believe who's over here!' When he heard it was me, he rushed home. By the time he got there, I was hysterical, crying about this guy and telling Julia about how he'd dumped me. Noel said he had a single friend he'd really like me to meet. I said that I really couldn't meet anyone right then because I was just a basket case. I didn't want to date. He insisted that he call his friend David, and we would all go out together and have fun and that it would take my mind off things. I went. Noel monopolized the conversation the entire evening. I didn't really care, but I thought it was a little rude.

"Noel was a manufacturer's rep for home entertainment products, and he needed someone to demonstrate them. I was off for the summer, and he offered me much more than the going rate to do the presentation. I showed up for work, and he had invited the blind date to meet me for lunch. It turned out that Noel wanted to take me out for breakfast and didn't really want me to work. Two hours later Dave showed up to take me to lunch, and the three of us went out. Every time Dave wanted to be with me, Noel seemed to be right behind. Now he had a license to call me every day because I was working for him. He started to show up at my doorstep constantly. He was always telling me he loved me and that he wanted to be with me and that he was unhappily married. I would listen to his story and then I would tell him to leave. I had no interest in him whatsoever and I was still dating his friend, David. One night he came to my house and told me I could learn to love him. He wouldn't leave, so I threw a shoe at him and told him to get out. He left but called the next day. This went on for about a year, and I started to like the attention. If he went two or three days without calling me, or if he went away on business, I would start to miss the phone calls. So as much as I was protesting that I couldn't stand him, I kind of missed the attention, and I was still in love with the guy who dumped me.

"Then I agreed to dinners. One night we went out to a clandestine dinner at a restaurant. Finally we kissed, and it progressed into mad, passionate kissing. One night we made love. He was an animal, and I was instantly hooked sexually. He loves women and he loves sex. That's how it all started. Slowly but surely the affair began and we were sneaking around.

"He was not happily married at the time, but I'm not so sure that if I hadn't been in his life, he would have left. His wife drank a lot and was verbally abusive. They had lost whatever it was that they had in common. She became 100 percent children-oriented and made no time for him. He started to resent it and screw around—I was not his first.

"It was a nightmare—it took about a year for him to leave his wife. He kept telling me he was going to leave: next month, next year—but he never did. We'd been sneaking around for two years. One year when nothing happened, and now another year where we were into this affair, and then he finally did it. He left. He had two very close friends who knew he was unhappy, and they knew me. I think they tried to talk him into leaving. It's not that they wanted him to be with me, but it was something he had wanted to do for a long time. Now he had a reason to leave, so they were really pursuing it. He now had another woman to go to.

"So he finally told his wife and kids that he was leaving. He is a people pleaser, and to this day I cannot imagine how he had the strength to do it. He's a yes-man and never argued, he never fought with her; he just quietly did what he wanted. I don't think he ever really expressed his total unhappiness to her. I'm not so sure she ever knew how miserable he was, even though she used to yell at him and close up the kitchen if he came in later than he was supposed to with business.

"So he finally told her and moved out and got an apartment. A friend of his owned the building. So now we were sneaking around there because he didn't want his wife to know. Then, all of a sudden, my former roommate called and said, 'I've been instructed to call and tell you that Noel has gone back to my sister.' I went crazy! I had no idea it was coming, because he's not a communicator. If he'd been getting pressure or awful things were happening, he never told me about it. I called her house and asked for him. She put him on the phone. I yelled at him and said I couldn't believe it. He came to see me and told me that a lot of things were going on and he couldn't take the pressure. His wife made him promise that he wouldn't communicate with me.

"His best friend called and asked me to meet him for a drink at this restaurant. At the same time, he had called Noel and asked him to meet him for a drink at the same restaurant. He wanted the two of us to talk. So we sat down, and his friend said, 'Noel, tell her how you feel about her.' So he did. Then he said to me, 'You tell him how you feel.' Then he said, 'He's having a time that is hard for you to understand because you are the woman waiting for this to happen.' This was October. I looked at Noel and said that if I was still by myself on New Year's Eve, he could forget about ever seeing me again.

"Two days before New Year's Eve he was at my house. That was the beginning of our relationship.

"He pursued me and I pushed him away. But when you want to justify things that you do that are wrong, you find reasons to justify it. I stopped kicking him out, and I made excuses like, 'Well, he's not very happy,' so I make excuses for what I do. It was the wrong thing to do. He was married—I knew her. I even liked her, so it's almost the same thing as screwing a friend, as far as I'm concerned. But at that point—and this is the sick part—I was alone, I loved the attention, and I was becoming attracted to him. So I made some justifications for why I was doing what I was doing.

"A very good friend of mine did basically the same thing, and she has no guilt over it whatsoever. I feel guilty. She's friendly with the ex-wife, who has remarried. They share holidays and everything. The wife is so happy not to have him.

"Julia went crazy. She came over to his apartment to visit him one night, and we were upstairs making love. He answered the door and she came into the living room. I was hiding underneath the bed. He got her out of the house, and suddenly she started smashing into all the cars in the parking lot.

"I want to tell you how I met the kids. One night the doorbell rang, and I heard, 'Hello, is my daddy there?' His wife had taken the kids, put them in the car, and said, 'Do you want to meet the whore your father is fucking?' She dropped them off in front of the building, told them what buzzer to ring, and drove off. They came into the apartment; you can imagine how I felt. Noel called his attorney and tried to negotiate how to get the kids back. A few hours later his wife was pounding on all the doors in the building, yelling, 'Everybody, there's a fucking whore living here!' She went nuts, and you know, at this point I think I would too, in her position. All these years she still hates me. You know, I don't blame her."

☙ ☙ ☙

Noel and Diane were married. Noel died of a heart attack when Diane was pregnant with their first child.

IN HER OWN WORDS: A WOMAN WHO STRAYED

EDNA, AGE SIXTY-ONE, SAYS:

"When I met Fred, I was forty years old and had been divorced for three years. My children were thirteen and fifteen, and they lived with me. A real "affair" would have been an unworkable situation. Maybe if I had been stronger and more confident, I could have handled it. My daughter used to just sit and stare at him with this great, stony face. After all, my children had learned in Sunday school 'Don't mess around with someone else's spouse.' But now he's just a fact of life and a part of my life, and he has been for twenty-one years.

"Fred had been married for seventeen years and had four children. I was his second affair, and I think he was ready to leave his marriage when I met him on a job interview. I didn't take the job with him because I felt an immediate attraction. Shortly after, I was invited to a dinner party with some friends, and he was there alone. Fred's wife was in Florida for the winter, and he was 'baching it.' That really was the beginning. We talked about all sorts of things—movies we liked, books we were reading. I knew he was married, but I guess I found it kind of exciting because I didn't know what was going to happen. The relationship flourished because his wife was gone from January until May. When she came back, he told her about us. He had talked to me about getting married, and I had said no. He was unhappy and wanted to get out of the marriage. I could not have handled the situation at that time because of my children. My son would have been telling him, 'Don't boss me around because you're not my father.' I didn't feel strong enough to handle it. The marriage wouldn't have lasted a year.

"Once his wife knew I wasn't going to ask him to leave her, she was okay. Interestingly enough, I think it was a relief to her, which is hard to explain. She wasn't that upset because she felt she was off the hook and didn't have to worry about pleasing him. He was there for family functions—he's very loyal. Because of that the tension eased, and then she got stronger and came out of it a lot better. He was a more relaxed, happy guy because of it. She kept her family and her social standing. I didn't want to get married. It worked for all of us. As unbelievable as it sounds, it was many years before anybody in the community had the least idea. A couple of times we were seen having dinner together, but everyone knew his wife was away and they just thought of me as a friend of the family.

"His wife is always very friendly when she sees me. I've had dinner with both Fred and his wife and their children. Three of his children are genuinely fond of me now that they are mature adults. I think they appreciated the fact that I didn't screw up their lives. To this day the youngest child still wishes I would drop off the face of the earth. She doesn't hate me as much as she can't understand why her mother tolerated it. I went to all the children's weddings as a 'friend of the family.' I didn't get to sit in the second pew, but I was there. My kids like him, they think he's good to their mom, and they know I'm not distressed. If anything ever happened to him, I'm sure his wife would call me.

"They get along great now. He has enormous respect for her, and he's fond of her; she's the mother of his children.

"I never seriously dated anyone else because from the time I got involved with Fred, I was involved emotionally. During hurricanes and surgeries I think about being married to Fred. Mostly, I'm happy. Holidays are really family times, and my children are always with me.

"Since I moved from Boston to Palm Beach, we see each other less—about once every six weeks for a few days—and we go on trips together. That's okay with me; we talk all the time. The worst part for me is financial. Fred's wife is better off than I am financially, but he does send a small check every month. He's not as social a person as I am, so I can go out and do things and see my friends. He's not a guy that needs a lot of friends or parties. His wife knows where he is, and she can always call if she needs to talk to him. She calls only for very good reasons. I would miss him very much if something happened to him.

"I think because of me Fred is able to get along with his wife better. I don't know if his wife was ever really sexual or not. They had three children right in a row, and when the fourth one came, I think she just said, 'That's it.' If she had been interested, I think she got turned off. When I met him, he was very unhappy. When he became more relaxed, because he was content and happy with me, he got along with his wife better and he was easier to live with. It took this great pressure off her, and she could relax and enjoy him as a friend, and he could enjoy her. I probably made the marriage. And it wasn't putting pressure on me. At the time we met, if my kids had been away at college, I probably would have married him, but by the time they did leave, we were comfortable.

"The bottom line is, it works for everybody and there's room for everybody. I love when he comes to visit, and I love to dress up and have him tell me I look nice. Sometimes I imagine how his obituary will read, 'He leaves his wife, his children, his grandchildren . . . and Edna!'"

🌿 🌿 🌿

Edna is a lovely, attractive, articulate, and educated woman. In no way does she fit the stereotype of the "other woman." And yet she is. Everyone involved claims to be comfortable with this arrangement.

WOMEN MEN STRAY *FROM*

My husband and I had a small dinner party recently and invited several of our friends. One couple asked if we would mind if they brought along their houseguest, an old friend who was visiting from out of town. They told us that Sally was in the middle of a very bad divorce, and they didn't want to leave her alone. Absolutely, no problem, we all agreed.

When Sally showed up, she'd obviously had one cocktail too many. In a very loud voice she proceeded to vent at all of us—strangers—about the fact that her husband had left her through no fault of her own, and she was still in shock. She claimed that both she and her husband were products of the "Ken-and-Barbie" generation, and all her husband wanted was a Barbie-doll collectible. She said that he couldn't deal with her success or ability to think as a woman. She talked well into the night, and no one got a word in edgewise. She said she was writing a book about the fact that men in the nineties are extremely intimidated by successful career women, and as a direct result they become impotent. She would title the book *When Ken Goes Limp!*

Sally considered herself a victim of the times and of changing expectations within relationships. After everyone had gone, I asked my husband, a practically angst-free man who loves just about everybody, what he thought. He was very turned off by Sally, whom he referred to as "aggressively insecure and thoroughly obnoxious." Perhaps she needed to tone it down a bit for her husband to adjust. Sally's friend, Joe, and his wife were not surprised by the divorce. "I love Sally," Joe said. "But, frankly, I don't know how her husband stayed as long as he did."

CAN YOU STRAY-PROOF YOUR HUSBAND?

Two of the most important things you can do to prevent your husband from straying are to trust very few of the women he spends much time with, and to take nothing for granted—especially him! As we've seen, men seem to stray more because of availability than for any other reason.

DOUGLAS, A THIRTY-SEVEN-YEAR-OLD ARTIST, SAYS:

"Most of the time I don't think men are looking for a certain type of woman—they're just looking to meet a woman. A lot of times it's who you meet, not who you're out looking for. Women think a lot of times that men have it so easy meeting women, asking them out and going out with them. A lot of times that's not true. What you get is what you get! I may meet fifty women and ask some of them out and probably get turned down by the majority. It's who you meet and who you eventually end up with more than who you're looking for. Some men may have fantasies—for example, he might really like voluptuous blonds, but that doesn't mean he's going to end up straying with a voluptuous blond."

🌿 🌿 🌿

You have to decide whether you will let him stray—or whether you'll work at making him want to stay. It's ridiculous to think he will look at no other women for thirty or forty years. Develop a sophisticated understanding of what motivates him *and* you. Whom he strays with may be directly related to his reason for straying. Is he looking to feel young in midlife? Does he want someone to pay attention and listen to him, or is he looking for a spousal replacement? More often than not an affair offers new, fun sex, unmarred by the realities of everyday life.

You can't avoid every situation or prevent every possibility of your husband straying, but you can make sure that he doesn't need to look elsewhere—outside your marriage—for what he needs.

"What is it I got that makes them twitch?"

☞ MARILYN MONROE

☞ PART TWO

Why Men Stay

ANThoNy:

"I knew she was the one. I like the way
she makes me feel about myself."

CHAPTER SEVEN

The Results Are In . . .

People are always asking couples whose marriage has endured at least a quarter of a century for the secret of success. Actually, it is no secret at all. I am a forgiving woman. Long ago, I forgave my husband for not being Paul Newman.

☞ ERMA BOMBECK

IT MAY COME AS NO SURPRISE that the reasons most men stay committed in a relationship are the very same reasons they committed initially. He's happy and in love, and she's still his best friend. The elements have not changed. The love, the companionship, and the great sex are still there. They stay when they're happy and satisfied and feel good about themselves. Men look to their wives for encouragement and ego support. They like frequent pats on the back.

DAVE, SECOND MARRIAGE:

"I chose to be with my wife, so that's why I like to be with her. We don't have any children and I know what a strain that is for a lot of marriages. I wouldn't want my personal happiness to come in second place. The kid thing can kind of take over, and the man-woman relationship just slides."

🖉 🖉 🖉

SURVEY RESULTS

I asked several hundred men with diversified demographics, ages twenty-one to seventy-nine, to fill out a questionnaire regarding why they stayed or strayed in their relationships, and what advice they would give to women to keep their men from straying. The answers are amazingly similar. I also inquired if they equated marriage with monogamy. A big surprise from both the stayers and the strayers is that 99 percent of men do equate marriage with monogamy.

Men also gave their personal secrets for a successful marriage.

GAVIN, A FIFTY-SEVEN-YEAR-OLD ATTORNEY,

SUMMED IT UP:

"Have respect for yourself and the institution of marriage, work at problem solving, never stop growing, and take the time to be as tastefully glamorous as you can."

🖉 🖉 🖉

DEREK, THIRTY-SEVEN, SAYS:

"Be naughty and trampy sometimes. Role-playing can be great. Keep it interesting, whatever it takes—and oral sex, of course. Often."

🖉 🖉 🖉

ANDY, FORTY-TWO, SAYS:

"Let him enjoy his own interests if they don't involve anything harmful to your relationship, and pursue yours with the same conditions."

🐾 🐾 🐾

JOSH, AGE FORTY-SIX, SAYS:

"Make time for your spouse—listen and hear—keep one eye partially closed. And don't let your ego get in the way!"

🐾 🐾 🐾

THEIR MOST COMMON REASONS FOR STAYING

1. A lifelong commitment of love
2. Genuine happiness
3. She loves him and makes him feel good
4. Fear of AIDS
5. Family upbringing
6. It works
7. Fear of being caught
8. Fear of the unknown
9. Children
10. Family responsibilities
11. Religion
12. He's lazy
13. He wouldn't want to get paid back in spades
14. It's the path of least resistance
15. He can't afford to leave

ARMAND, FIFTY, SECOND MARRIAGE:

"AIDS changed my lifestyle. I never really worried about getting it, but it was this major topic when I went out with someone. I used to think it was something made up by the 'moral majority' to get people to stop screwing around. Slowly, it became a realistic concern. No woman was worth dying for. That's why I got married and settled down."

🌿 🌿 🌿

CHARLES, TWENTY-FIVE-YEAR VETERAN OF THE
INSTITUTION:

"I like to think that the positive reasons are the ones you stay for, not the easy ones. The best love is a lasting love."

🌿 🌿 🌿

I asked the men I interviewed for any advice they had for women to keep their men from straying. Here's what they said:

- "You've got to be friends above all, or your marriage won't last."
- "Frequent, great sex."
- "Emotional attention."
- "Keep it interesting."
- "Spontaneous oral sex (anytime, anywhere, often)."
- "Be your husband's best friend."
- "Make the relationship work."
- "Stay in shape."
- "Make it exciting."
- "Don't bitch; trust."

- "Spend time with one another."
- "Don't take each other for granted; it brings boredom."
- "Talk to each other; don't just speak to each other."
- "Remain a wife when you become a mother."
- "Communicate, communicate."
- "Give respect, responsibilities, and freedom as long as it does not hurt the relationship."
- "Don't tie him down; give him enough freedom to understand you trust him; then he will always trust you."

The best marriage I see is Ted Turner and Jane Fonda's. But they work at it all the time. I don't know that I'm prepared to work that much.

☞ LARRY KING

They also cited what they thought were the most important elements in a great marriage:

- Trust and love
- Mutual respect
- Excellent and frequent sex
- Sense of humor
- Not letting disagreements blow up into full-scale arguments
- Being honest with yourself
- Loyalty
- Prudent use of family finances
- Kindness

- Willingness to apologize
- Friendship
- Being a team player
- Being able to spend time with one another
- Common commitment to staying together

MIDGE, MARRIED SIXTY YEARS:

"Always admit when you're wrong and never point out when you're right! That's my secret to a happy marriage."

🌿 🌿 🌿

Midge certainly must have done something right for her union to last sixty years. It might be a good idea to reread these lists periodically. Just as a reminder, *remember* maintenance is the key issue in any lasting partnership if you want your spouse to stay.

LES, TWENTY-SIX:

"I think that the most important thing to keep your man from straying is to make it very clear that you trust him not to; that it would be a betrayal."

🌿 🌿 🌿

In Their Own Words: Conversations with Stayers

Buzzy, fifty-four, second marriage, business/law-school grad, says:

"I've been married for three years and nine days. The reason I know that is because my wife is very smart. That's one of the reasons why I married her, I love her, and I'm staying with her. We got married on July 11, which is 7-Eleven. I didn't think anything about it until she said, 'You will never be able to drive down a street without seeing one of those stores. Every one will remind you for the rest of your life of your anniversary.'

"I equate marriage with monogamy. I've been approached by very attractive women. I wear a wedding ring. I was tempted on occasion, but then I know that it really isn't worth it. I think I've reached a point in my life, age, and self-knowledge where I know I would feel terrible, so it wouldn't be worth it. After that, it was just kind of flattering, and I was proud of myself because I actually resisted, which was wonderful.

"There's a favorite restaurant/hangout near where I live, and my wife and I frequently go together. So people know who I am. This girl comes in there frequently. She's kind of wild, the way she dresses. She's very intelligent and has had a very interesting life; she's in her early thirties. She's very attractive but she's kind of wacky. There are lots of serious diseases out there. This girl was very, very aggressive. She approached me and said, 'I've always been attracted to older men,' and then we had a conversation about other things, and she said, 'There's something about gray hair that just drives me crazy. I love gray hair.' She had the flattery down pat. It was hard not to succumb, but I didn't.

"Some men stray for the fun of it, and they have no intention of leaving their wives, and the other category is looking for a relationship. Men stray because they're looking for a diversion or relief."

🌿 🌿 🌿

F. J., SEVENTY-NINE, MARRIED FIFTY-FIVE YEARS, SAYS:

"Firstly and very seriously, I do consider marriage to be a permanent commitment between two people. It should be entered into in good faith and with the expectation that consummation of the union will result in the arrival of children in the future, and involve rearing them in an atmosphere of love and commitment to each other. This is of tremendous importance in terms of their future emotional stability.

"It appears to be a fact that our contemporary society and its morality are structured so that they encourage defections from the marriage commitment. It supposes that we are unwilling, or intellectually unable, to enter into lifelong commitments. Yet I have been married to the same woman for fifty-five years. We met when she was seventeen and I was twenty. So many years later, having raised six children of our own, we are the proud and happy grandparents of fifteen grandchildren and six great-grandchildren. We remain committed to one another, and best friends.

"Life was never easy in the first twenty years of our marriage, either from an economic point of view or from physical and mental aspects of our daily lives. In many ways it was not what one would call well planned. Planning, to the extent there was any, was confined to purely mundane matters. During this period of our lives there were strains associated with our continually growing family and our limited finances. We survived the stresses, and I believe we're the stronger for it. Throughout this period I looked for and received constant support from my partner, who almost never lost her patience or sense of humor.

"As it happens, we had a similar religious background but do not consider that it was necessarily the compelling factor in the longevity of our marriage. Certainly it was not a divisive nor a disruptive factor. Fortunately, we did not have to deal with infidelity or constant bickering with each other. We consciously and constantly sought to create an atmosphere designed to provide a feeling of love and security for our children. Our hope is that we did provide such an environment.

"I look upon my wife of fifty-five years as a person of many talents and possessed of intelligence and stability. If temperament and purpose are rare in our world today, where it often seems that superficiality reigns supreme and quality is overlooked, when I consider the many roles our life has required her to play, I am amazed at her proficiency. To name a few, consider wife and sexual partner, mother, teacher, protector, and mentor to six children, and last, but not least, a social being in her community. I feel that I have been the recipient of a great gift for which I am eternally grateful."

❦ ❦ ❦

C. J., SEVENTY-SIX, HIS WIFE OF FIFTY-FIVE YEARS, ON HER
FORMULA FOR SUCCESSFUL MARRIAGE:

"I always put my husband first. The kids will grow up and go their own way if you raised them correctly. Your relationship is the most important thing. Oh, yeah, and don't point out when he's wrong."

❦ ❦ ❦

If your relationship is as stable and rewarding as these stayers'—you should feel lucky and grateful as well. But never start taking your relationship for granted—a lifetime of commitment and marital fidelity requires a lifetime of attention and effort.

CHAPTER EIGHT

Sense and Sensitivity: How to Turn the Strayer into a Stayer

DALE, FIFTY-TWO, FORMER STRAYER:

"I've trolled with the best and the worst, and I've slept with their wives, but I have given it up. I actually feel liberated. Perhaps I should have tried it sooner . . . nah!!!

On why he changed:

"Life turned me old and gray, and I no longer have an appetite for prospecting."

🌿 🌿 🌿

YOUR PARTNER HAS STRAYED—or you're afraid he might. But you want to make your marriage work, or you would not be reading this chapter! Start this instant. Get rid of all your ammunition and baggage and muster your most positive attitude. Concentrate on the good times. As one woman said at her anniversary party when asked how she got through fifty years of marriage, "With a very short memory." Her advice to other women, "Don't carry a grudge!"

Start to think and act the way you did when you first started dating. No, you do not have to greet your man swathed in plastic wrap at day's end, but you are going to have to make some heavy concessions. Men are high maintenance—and you may have to make some changes to keep their interest. Approach it as you would a new job or business, with attention, dedication, and action.

If you have decided to remain in the relationship, you *can* make it work. Infidelity need not be the end of the world (although it may feel that way) or the end of your relationship. You can turn it around to a new beginning, and it can be better than ever—a celebration. Get rid of the old problems. Who said that the definition of insanity is doing the same thing over and over and expecting change? Get counseling, work on it. Renew your vows.

I had been divorced for seventeen years before I met my husband. I had a number of marriage proposals along the way, and hundreds of dates. I always noticed that the men I dated who had been married before behaved very differently from, and were more tolerant, less critical, and more polite than, the guys who had never been married. I had been seeing a man who'd been married for sixteen years. His wife had been having an affair with his friend, and it was she who had initiated divorce proceedings. Nevertheless, when she saw her ex-husband's picture with me in the paper at different social events around Boston, she decided she wanted him back. "I didn't train him for sixteen years to make another woman happy!" she said. I thought, "*Train* him. What is he, a puppy?" But over time, and observing many married couples, I have come to understand what she meant. He knew enough to call at designated times of the day, not to make plans with "the boys" that didn't include her, and if he was going to be home later than 6 p.m., he would give her advance notice. He was also magnificently dressed. But none of this happened instantly. It evolved slowly over time. Remember: men are trainable, women are adaptable. You must have patience.

SEXUAL COMPATIBILITY

Like it or not, the single biggest reason men stray is sex. There's either not enough at home or it's not interesting enough.

If you are indeed committed to the marriage, you can get him to stay home where he belongs. Make him feel important. He needs to be appreciated even when he doesn't deserve it.

Keep the communication going and be honest. Work hard to reawaken romance and love in your relationship.

HELEN, FORTY-SIX, SAYS:

"Look at all the self-help books out there now on sexual relationships. Look at all the videos on sexual relationships: how to recharge your sex life, sensual products promising pleasure, etcetera. They're all over the place; they're very prominent. If people didn't get bored with each other sexually, you wouldn't have these books and things so available.

"Everyone now who has a brain is monogamous because of fear of AIDS. Your husband's straying could be a wake-up call. It could be thought of as an opportunity to look at the relationship and see what's missing, what's not working. It's unreasonable and naive of people to think that in their lifetime of a marriage, twenty to fifty years, that person they are with is going to be the only person they're ever going to be attracted to. It's very sad that you can't act out as we did in the sixties if we were attracted to somebody. In the sixties and seventies we had the attitude that we could sleep with somebody, still be their best friend the next day, and not have any expectations from that. Now we can't act that out. It puts a great deal of frustration on everybody involved.

"This is the first time in the history of men and women in relationships where people are more monogamous than they ever have been before, except for the Puritan days. Any famous person that you've ever read about always had a 'lover.' They didn't call it an affair, they called it 'lovers,' even presidents of our country.

"I'm pretty confident that my husband wouldn't stray. I take care of him; I give him what he needs emotionally and sexually. I also know that he's the kind of man who cares how the woman he's with looks, and I do a lot of maintenance. I do my exercises every day, not only because it's important to make me feel good, but because of how I look. The better I look, the more erections he's going to get. I know my husband would love me even if I gained a lot of weight, but he isn't going to be as turned on by me. A lot of women decide, 'Okay, I've had my kids and I'm involved in the community and my career.' The husband isn't demanding sex, so they think he's not interested, so they're not interested. They don't know that he may be sleeping with somebody on the side, and if they don't recognize that, then by the time the other woman starts replacing the wife, that's what the problem is—if you don't recognize the warning signs and do something, confront him—you just keep thinking that his indifference is his indifference rather than thinking 'Is he not interested because he's getting it someplace else?' When he's not interested in sex with you, that should be one of the first warning signs. That is the wake-up call! The first thing should be, 'We're not sleeping together—why? Something's wrong with our sex life—why? Let's make it work because it's so much fun.'

"When a man and a woman have been sleeping together for years, the emotional thing has to start to fall apart too. If you drift apart sexually, you're bound to drift apart emotionally."

🌱 🌱 🌱

It is important to learn to communicate your sexual needs. Are you able to tell him what feels good and what doesn't? Share your fantasies with your spouse, be they vibrators, videos, or whatever they are. Communication is the art of the relationship, which is the art of love. Don't be afraid to show or tell him if he's touching you in a spot that's not giving you any satisfaction. Guide his hands where you want them, and tell him it's wonderful. Don't sit and think, "If he would only do this," because you're afraid of hurting his feelings and damaging his ego. Men want you to do this because when it's over, they see that you are very satisfied and that makes them happy. They know the difference when you're really satisfied.

Even though a man loves his wife, he'll be more satisfied with the strayee who will let him know how to satisfy her; he will feel so rewarded that he knows how to please a woman. That will make him feel that he is good as a man sexually, and that's why he's straying. Take a look at the world's oldest profession and why men go to prostitutes. These women don't experience climax with every customer—they couldn't—so they fake it, but they say the right thing so he feels it. A wife still has to say the right things to make the man feel like a man. Be verbal. When you fake it, you still have to say the right things.

TED, TWENTY-EIGHT, SAYS:

"Prostitutes satisfy the male ego. That's all it is. It's not the screw. The wife is saying, 'Hurry up, I've got to do the laundry.' My wife never comes on to me. She never comes in while I'm taking a shower and jumps in and starts washing me. I always have to be the initiator."

🌿 🌿 🌿

ALLISON, FORTY-THREE, SAYS:

"Be sexy in the bedroom; don't get fat and let yourself go. When you see pictures of so many women twenty years ago, they're unrecognizable. They were thin and had gorgeous long hair and were well put together. You see them today and they're fat, they dress terribly and they have short, permed hair. My philosophy is if you look back to when you dated and how hard you worked to turn people's heads, it's a good measure not to lose sight of. Sometimes I wish I could let myself go and not care about how I looked, but that same day my husband may get on a plane and some gorgeous woman will sit next to him and be throwing herself at him. If he left me that morning with the old robe, my hair sticking out, and bad breath, he may take that road. You never know what's going to happen, and there are so many women out there who are aggressive—I've seen what goes on. Bottom line— you can't get too comfortable. Last week my husband's partner was on a plane, and some girl sitting next to him asked him if he wanted to go to the bathroom to 'do it'! This guy is very conservative, straitlaced, and married to a beautiful woman. He said no. See how easily it happens? The availability and the opportunity are ever present."

❦   ❦   ❦

FRANK, FIFTY-FOUR, SAYS:

"There are many women who don't care. They're perfectly happy if their husband has a mistress, because that's one less thing they have to be bothered with. They don't really care to meet his needs; their needs are being fulfilled monetarily if not emotionally, and maybe they're getting emotional fulfillment through their children. There are so many women who, once they're married and have a family, the family is everything, not the husband. It's really important to keep that marriage strong and alive rather than just being a mother and seeing him only as a father to the children. Very often that's what happens. That's why so many marriages break up. The man always wants to feel special. He wants to feel that he's got that one soul mate. I do too. I want that one person in my life that no matter what, I can turn to her. Maybe she won't always understand every feeling that I have. Men want that feeling. They want to know that they are the most important thing in your life. You have to set boundaries."

🌿 🌿 🌿

To love oneself is the beginning of a lifelong romance.

☞ Oscar Wilde

Becoming a Renaissance Woman

By expanding your horizons and maturing as an adult, you are going to get out of any ruts you have unconsciously fallen into. The goal is to become a multidimensional woman. Not only will your spouse appreciate the new you, but you will probably fall in love with yourself all over again. The object is to be part wife, part sex goddess, and part interesting human being. An interested person is an interesting person. Be aware of what's going on in the world and live life to the fullest.

When he comes home at the end of the day, you will have paid attention to your appearance. You will have thrown out your old, ratty bathrobe. You won't greet him with complaints about the plumber or the kids. Instead you will have some quiet time alone and focus on him. Your attitude will be infectious. Remember that you can change only your own behavior, not his. Your basic aim here is to reprogram your husband through pattern developing. He won't be able to get enough of you, and straying will be the furthest thing from his mind.

YOUR PERSONAL BEST

In order to accomplish your goal, you are going to be the best you can be. First, you're going to do a personal checklist and ask yourself the following questions:

1. Have I gained more than twenty pounds since I was married?
2. Have there been any other significant changes in my appearance?
3. Have I experienced a drop in sex drive?
4. Is my response to his amorous advances one of reckless abandon or of "no time like the present"?
5. Am I as interesting a person as when he met me?

Men are visual and are attracted to youthful, healthy-looking females. Clean, bouncy, shiny hair, white teeth, smooth skin, and a body in reasonably good shape without excess lumps and bumps are the turn-ons. It's important to make the most of your assets and keep them in good working order; this adds to your confidence and sense of well-being. Toning and trimming are ego building. You feel better about things and are more enthusiastic about life.

THE TURN-ONS	THE TURN-OFFS
■ Sexual spontaneity (attack or seduce him at an unlikely time)	■ "Mappies"—male-bashing, angry professional women
■ Femininity	■ Abrasiveness
■ A positive attitude	■ A negative attitude
■ Staying in shape	■ Fat
■ Good humor	■ Smoking
■ Healthy skin, teeth and hair	■ Sloppiness
■ Independence	■ Nagging
■ A sense of goodwill	■ Giving orders
■ Kissing, hugging and touching	■ Criticizing
■ Interesting conversationalist	■ Being too tired or impatient to listen to his problems (he'll take them to his secretary)
	■ Constant venting and complaining
	■ Snoring
	■ Being too tired for sex
	■ Referring to your spouse as "Mom" or "Dad" (you'll start thinking of them as your parent)
	■ Total dependency
	■ Mud masks
	■ Nose hair
	■ Shower caps (they'll remind him of his grandmother)

Begin your own wellness program. Food and activity impact the quality of your life. Start out your day with calisthenics and daily stretches. It's ego building and you will feel better about things. You will have more spring in your step and more enthusiasm about life.

1. Get your body in good shape. You feel better when you look better. The added bonus will be all those happy endorphins rushing in and killing off any depression.
2. Take a class; learn to do something new—like play a musical instrument or speak a foreign language.
3. Become culturally aware. Take classes in art appreciation. Learn about ballet and opera.
4. Volunteer for at least a few hours a month in your community.
5. Make a concerted effort to have some income of your own.
6. Develop your senses—experience the scents around you, be the fragrances of flowers or delicious aromas of cooking. Look at the sunset and the color of the sky. Be aware of the sense of touch.
7. Keep a sense of humor. Most men agreed that a sense of humor is crucial to any relationship.

The key to happiness is, of course, to learn to develop yourself and be your own person. Several things factor into this equation. Working outside the home expands your network of associates, thereby making you a more interesting person. It also provides you with independence that only your own salary will bring—money brings freedom. The lack of personal income makes you beholden to your spouse and diminishes your position to one of subordination. It is equally important to develop and continue on your journey to becoming a mature, full human being.

You are going to be the best you can be, just like when you were going for the commitment. If need be, think back to when you were first dating—when you cared how you looked and what you wore. You kept up your appearance and worked at being sexy. You were his lover, not his mother. You have to make a conscious effort to maintain this kind of relationship. And, remember, you don't need to know every single thing about your spouse. Ownership is smothering. Give him a little space and consider doing the following:

- Be a little mysterious—don't tell him your every thought.
- Be exciting, not predictable.
- Have a sense of adventure.
- Live for today; don't obsess about the future.
- Don't vent and complain.
- Don't give him the third degree.
- Don't ask too many personal questions.

THE BUSINESS OF MARRIAGE

My husband entered several corporate-sales training programs after he graduated from college in the late sixties. He worked principally in sales while studying art and painting part-time. He is an accomplished artist whose medium is oil and very large formats. When someone is considering buying one of his paintings, he quickly squelches any problems of "It's so big, how will we ship it?" or "I'm not sure I can afford it now." He offers the prospective buyer the simplest deal: charge it, pay in monthly installments, or we'll bill you. And he doesn't lose the deal because of complications regarding delivery; he has an arrangement with a packaging company. The best sales in his gallery take place when he is there.

My husband amazes me because he always ends up happy and content with his business deals and contracts, unlike just about everybody else I know. Sometimes I think he's too generous and pays an employee too high a salary. Other times I'm astonished at his trust and the fact that he always gives a person the benefit of the doubt. He responds by saying, "I'm not greedy." And then he gives his famous definition of a good deal: "A good deal is when it's a good deal for you and a good deal for me." If one person is unhappy, it's not a good deal. The longer we're together, the more I see how this applies to so many aspects of life, and especially to relationships.

Marriage is a business contract you enter into with shared visions and objectives. It's about teamwork and continuous improvement toward your long-term goals. This involves planning and cooperation by both parties in order to achieve team satisfaction. Relationships involve personal integrity first. Each partner must be mobilized to address specific issues and use problem-solving skills. Both partners must be motivated toward the fulfillment of a common purpose. This can be achieved only if both actively participate in shaping the way the relationship works.

Support, participation, and commitment are the hallmarks of the happily married. In order to succeed, you must learn to work effectively in the team and achieve the common purpose! As the marriage tries to maintain a balance, either you build an effective team or you fail. Only you can decide if you want to make the marriage work.

Whenever we are in a business situation, buying or selling furniture, a TV, or even a car, he always quotes his famous three rules of sales and follow-up that he learned in the corporate sales seminars:

THE RULES OF SELLING

1. Don't confuse selling with installing.
2. Keep it simple.
3. Ninety percent of business is being there.

These rules easily transfer to the marriage contract. Perhaps in your struggle to get your husband to commit, you followed the first rule in business: don't confuse selling with installing. It worked! You wanted to get the commitment, and you didn't want to confuse the deal with cumbersome details that might have scared him away. This is a very common mistake. Perhaps you neglected to mention that your ex-husband didn't pay child support, and now you're having financial difficulty. Or maybe you knew your mother would have to live with you, but you thought if you mentioned it, your fiancé wouldn't want the arrangement. You went for the commitment and nothing else mattered; you didn't want to confuse the issue with the facts. He may be resentful and feel duped now that you are, in reality, dealing with the problems you concealed.

We can effortlessly overwhelm ourselves by making every situation too complicated to handle. It's not always easy to process the changes that marriage brings, the reversals of our expectations. We are, after all, human beings with limitations. Remember the second rule: "keep it simple," by breaking down the large problems into small, solvable ones. And keep talking. Remember, you married your best friend.

The third rule, 90 percent of business is being there, is possibly the most important and will become more apparent as you continue to read this book. After the sale takes place, follow-up is essential. After all, how do you expect a close partnership to flourish if you don't spend enough time with your spouse? Would you try to run a business by not being there? Of course not! You have to stay on top of your relationship on a daily basis and be able to handle the constant problems that arise. If you're not there, he'll find someone who will be. Stay an active part of his life, and know what's going on in his daily activities. As a fun example, make an effort to participate in an activity together. Join a theater group. Learn to shoot pool. Join a choir or bowling league.

All people who are successful in relationships are good listeners. They hear and respond to what their friends and relatives are really saying. Train yourself to listen carefully; this is the key. You should have already created a friendly and trusting atmosphere in which your man feels free to converse with you honestly and confide in you freely. By listening to his comments and observing his body language, you will recognize the signals when he is having a problem before it's too late, before he turns to another woman for support. Problems have causes. Ask yourself, "Is he traumatized by turning forty?" Is there something you can do to boost his ego and make him feel more exciting? Let him know how important he is to you. Listen when he talks; laugh at his jokes as if it's the first time you heard them. Show overt signs of affection. Tell him you love him and think he's sexy. If you're in this for the long haul, you're going to have to make the effort.

STEPHANIE, THIRTY-EIGHT, SECOND MARRIAGE, SAYS:

"You have to work at it. Every day, twenty-four hours a day, it's a responsibility. It's like a game you have to play: How can I make things more exciting? Some things they respond to and some things they won't. But you have to always keep trying, because sex is overrated and it gets boring. You have to learn to accept that it isn't going to be hot sex, like when you first started dating. It's never going to be like that once you get past that stage. You can do things like skinny-dip in the pool together or make time and take an afternoon together. Wear something sexy even though it might not result in sex. At least it's a conscious effort, and it makes him feel good, and more important, it makes you feel good that you're doing everything you can. So if it doesn't work, it's not because you didn't try. It might not always end in fruition, but he can't just back off. I think the biggest line of bull is that we all want intimacy, when down deep, we all just want a good lay. Everybody needs it. In the meantime intimacy is the thing you can control.

"Being with someone older, I have to work even harder. People think that because I'm twenty years younger that it's easier, but, in reality, it's harder because I'm dealing with physiological things that happen to men as they get older. At the same time, I try to make him feel like a wonderful lover even though he's scared he's going to have a heart attack every time he has sex. It's constant ego reinforcement.

"Unfortunately, we don't take responsibility for ourselves. Men will block out everything to do what they want. Women make sure everybody's got what they want, and then they get to themselves. We're raised that way. I don't tell my husband half the stuff I do. The last thing I'm going to do is vent all over him when he comes home at the end of the day. I don't tell him how much everything costs. Then it becomes a control issue. You have to be realistic.

"My advice to other women is that it always starts with being happy with yourself, and, ideally, that entails living a healthy lifestyle. If you do that, it radiates already in the relationship, and then you're not dumping on him. Be responsible for your life, and expect men to respond to that. If they don't, then this isn't a person you can be intimate with. It does take two, even though there's always more responsibility for women to do more of the work. But you can fight this reality and never be happy, or you can learn how to incorporate it into your life.

"Too often women allow the children to become first in the relationship. I'm in a second marriage and I have a child, but I put my husband first, because my child is going to be gone at eighteen. I hope my husband will be with me for a long, long time. It's a constant challenge, because there are times that I have to tell my daughter that I'm going to be away for a week, and she doesn't like it. That's when you hire good child care and you leave, because if you don't—if you start not going on trips with your husband—it's a mistake. If I don't go, I make sure he's had the best lay before he goes. When he goes, I want him to be happy.

"You have to put your husband first. Too often I see marriages where the kid becomes the focus and the husband almost becomes the nonentity. There are things you can control in a relationship. We eat when my husband wants to eat. If my daughter can't wait that long, then I sit down with her and fix her something. I have dinner with my husband. I plan on being married to this person for the rest of my life.

"His point is, 'I've worked thirty years, and I finally found a woman that I'm in love with and want to be with and I want her to be with me.' And it's not an issue of 'I want you to stop everything and live your life through me.' It's 'I want you to be with me.' So I recognize that the thing that would damage my relationship right now is if I were to find a full-time job. The whole key is that he wants me to be with him, so I can't be offended by that. If he wants to take me out and have a two-hour lunch, I'll call a baby-sitter so that I can be with him. He says he always wanted to be with a woman he could take out to lunch, have a glass of wine with, and go home and take a nap together. He wants to be able to do that without having to hear, 'I have to pick up the kid or get back to the office.'

"Commitment is just beginning with marriage. It's a deep, zealous, almost religious feeling that guides you. It's not a big black cloud that hangs over you. I find it's something that tells you what's right and wrong. When you're committed, you know that sleeping with somebody else is wrong. That commitment guides you. That doesn't mean you can't think about it or fantasize about it, which is all very healthy, but that commitment is the thing that keeps you going straight instead of weaving in and out. Some people think it's okay to screw around because their spouse got heavier or smokes or some other reason. It's not okay. Because if you think it's okay, then there's no such thing as a relationship. If you're not happy and you don't want to be married, then get out, go forward.

"Women should not put up with men straying for any reason. As a gender, we need to be more demanding and say, 'I'm a valuable person, I should be treated like one.' The reason men stray with their secretary is that they spend a lot of time with each other, there's a bond, and, without sounding too condescending, women should act more like the secretary. Secretaries serve men, wait on them, anticipate their moods. They make things easy for them, rather than bitch and complain all the time. When a man loves you, he'll do the same! I've watched women with their husbands, and the transactions that take place are amazing. A married couple can be very nasty to each other, and yet they become so numb to it, they don't realize it.

"I really appreciate my husband. He's supportive even when I know it's killing him inside; he knows that to keep me, he's got to be understanding and give me some space. Maybe sometimes that's the value of second marriages. I picked the person who I thought would be loyal to me, and who I felt secure with. I also feel a very strong passion toward him and I'm very attracted to him. I didn't pick the right person the first time. With my first husband I didn't feel that passion, and I was always beating myself up for wanting something more, and for feeling I was being demanding."

🌾 🌾 🌾

A marriage, just like a business, operates most effectively when both members understand their duties and when they know who is responsible for each task—when one person doesn't suffocate the other, and good discussion and clear communication take place. You need to focus on each other and on the follow-through—on satisfying the needs of the customer.

Both partners should participate in decision making. Marriage is a collaborative effort based on a partnership and on a common set of goals and purposes. Both must accomplish certain tasks, from earning money to performing menial household jobs. The delegation of work and the division of labor must be understood by both partners. This can create discord if people are very set in their ways.

In order to be a successful and productive couple, each person will have to put up with the idiosyncrasies of the other. These can include something as petty as your squeezing the toothpaste from the wrong end or his leaving the toilet seat up. You must confront the issues of controlling and being controlled, competing and cooperating, success, failure, sharing, and mutual recognition of differences. You need to establish enduring patterns that define you as a two-person unit. Conflicts occur when unresolved issues are reawakened and (spousal) authority figures are symbolically equated with parents. The subordinate wife who is afraid to confront her husband, whom she suspects of straying, tries to ignore her painful feelings and feels helpless. This reaction is a defensive move on her part, which creates anxiety as she disavows the most troubling aspect of her marriage. The couple creates unconscious agreements as a defense against recognizing underlying problems inherent in achieving and maintaining collaboration. If you become sullen and resentful, you can reach a stalemate. A successful partnership cannot operate with power plays. You want to prevent greater problems. Conflicts may appear fairly mild at one point, but if you don't work through the issues, they can really flourish. What's your role? Are you the nurturer? Think about what you want and what you give. You might want to ask yourself, "What do I have to give to get what I want?"

FINANCES

Be aware of your man's financial commitments. Many men I spoke to complained that their wives took them for granted or spent too much money, creating undue pressure for them. Here, again, communication and cooperation are essential. Make sure you let him know that you don't take him for granted or just think of him as someone to pay the bills.

Try to communicate openly and honestly with your man about finances so that any complications can be dealt with early on and spending patterns negotiated. Stay aware of each other's expectations and attitudes regarding money.

Did you split the tab with him on dates but act shocked when he expected you to share expenses in your married life? It's time for an intelligent discussion of financial matters. Perhaps you want to be supported, and he thought he was getting into a dual-income situation. Remember, marriage is a long-term commitment and your mate's continued satisfaction as well as your own must be a concern.

Every man I interviewed said that money was not an issue when they were young and getting married for the first time. In second marriages, or later-life marriages, however, money becomes a significant factor. Jealousy can take over when there are things you would like but his parents or children from a past marriage are first to get the goodies. Again, expectations can be at odds—does he think of his income as "my money" or "our money"?

Set up financial meetings with your marital partner periodically to assess how you're doing. Sit down at a table and negotiate a budget. Discuss the spending patterns of both partners. Set up a special "fun" or vacation account, and both of you work toward filling it up.

DEALING WITH THE EX-WIFE

Your husband may not have made an emotional break with his former spouse. She calls him when the dog gets lost and when the dishwasher is broken. She calls him when she finds a spider in the bathtub. This creates considerable pressure on your relationship. She may tell him she needs additional money for the children or household expenses.

"If you don't pay the oil bill, *your* children will freeze to death this winter." She infuriates you and gets his attention. Of course, he doesn't want his children to freeze; he loves his kids and wants to take care of them. That's one of the reasons you fell in love with him. He's a responsible guy. You and your husband may argue about it (a victory for her!). You may be irate and think he's being manipulated by his ex-wife. You're right. But it serves no purpose to accuse him or get angry. It's more important to resolve the issue once and for all than to argue with your husband and try to get him to admit that you're right. Allowing his ex- to cause this kind of friction will increase her dependency, which will continue to cause problems in your relationship. Think about the options. You want her out of your life. You might be better off with his giving her more money on the condition that she manage it herself. This solution may be difficult for you financially, but it could be the best investment you ever made. Consider it a write-off. An additional bonus might be that your husband appreciates you for making the suggestion. What's it worth to you not to have to go through the same old hassle again? The bottom line is you want to help him to make the break.

A man's home may seem to be his castle on the outside;
inside it is more often his nursery.

☞ CLARE BOOTHE LUCE

Prenuptial Agreements

You live in a community-property state, and he insisted you sign a prenuptial agreement. Now you take care of the house; you may even chip in on the monthly mortgage payments. You start to think, Why should I, when my name isn't even on the deed? But, wait—you signed the agreement, right? Many men I spoke to complained that their wives "flip-flopped" after the ceremony took place. Perhaps you figured you'd sign now and worry about it later. But "later" came sooner than you expected, and now these complications must be dealt with.

Never forget that cooperation on both sides is essential in learning to communicate openly and honestly. A successful commitment occurs when both partners understand its purpose and its goals. Each must remain aware of the other's expectations and attitudes regarding money, and trickery should not enter into the picture.

Solution: build in a periodic review of your prenuptial agreement, to allow for changes in your financial situation.

Your Plan

Strategic planning in business is knowing where you want to be within a certain time frame and understanding what you have to do to get there. It's putting yourself in the best possible position in order to accomplish your objectives. This concept is also applicable to your marital relationship.

You wanted to be married; you chose your man. Some problems have occurred and you need to solve them. Now set a time limit for achieving your goal (say, six months to a year) and follow a clear strategy to accomplish your mission. Every thirty days review the status of your relationship just as you would review any personal goal.

Ask yourself, How much closer am I to solving the problems? What can I do to speed up the process?

Both partners should learn to cooperate with each other and use techniques that enable them to solve problems and work effectively as a team, thereby realizing their expectations. If your spouse refuses to cooperate in using these skills, influence him through your own example, and eventually he will come around. Keep in mind the following:

- Don't expect everything to work instantly.
- Don't ignore the changes that marriage brings—deal with them.
- Establish ground rules.
- Have frequent, open discussions.
- Respond to problems at the outset and plan to resolve them within a practical time frame.
- Find out and understand what caused the problem so it does not reoccur.
- Don't blame or fear.
- Acknowledge the needs and requests of each other.
- Define long-term strategies.

CHAPTER NINE

How Family Issues Can Affect Your Marriage

You, as an adult, must take responsibility for your life. Blame and accusations and name-calling serve no purpose and solve nothing. You may want to consider whether the union is worth saving. What are the problems, and are they solvable? Do you have insidious little battles, or huge blowouts? It's important to have a good fighting dynamic if you want to stay connected and resolve issues. Try to focus on what the real problem is. Make every effort to be objective. Can you and he benefit from outside help, such as going to a marriage counselor?

CONFLICT RESOLUTION

The ability to solve disputes can help a relationship endure. If you and your man cannot come to agreement about issues that create unhappiness when you are together, you may find yourselves going different ways.

Solving conflicts is not a magical gift; it is a learned skill. For this you will each need a pencil and a piece of paper. At a mutually agreed-upon time, sit down at a table and, one at a time, without interruption, air your views. Express your feelings with sentences that begin with "I feel" rather than "You do this" or "You should do that." "I feel" sentences are nonthreatening and nonhurtful to the other party.

While your man is speaking his mind, jot down any issues he brings up that you wish to address. When he makes a statement that translates into a problem that needs solving, such as "I feel annoyed when your kids are with you every weekend," jot it down. When he's finished speaking, it's your turn to speak without interruption, and his turn to write himself notes and jot down issues that need resolution.

When you have your lists, prioritize them from the most easily solved to the most difficult, knotty problems. Solve the easiest ones first. This will give you a feeling of success, raise your spirits, build a sense of teamwork, and provide the momentum to tackle the tough conflicts. For example, if it bothers him to take his car every time you go out, and if you don't mind taking your car occasionally, then you can come to an agreement to take turns driving, either on an alternate basis or with another plan that satisfies you both. If he doesn't like spending time with your children, though—save that for last. Let him know you are committed to solving the problems and that you'll stay at the table all night, if need be, to get things worked out. If there's an opportunity to inject humor into the discussion, go with it as long as it isn't at either person's expense. Keep the mood light and cooperative.

The thing to keep in mind is that it is easier to solve a bunch of little problems than a big mess that hasn't been divided into smaller issues. Try to keep the issues as small and manageable as possible, then approach them singly. If one does not resolve itself as easily as anticipated, then skip it, go on to another, and come back to it later.

Try to focus on the real problem and make every effort to be objective. Let him know you are committed to solving the problems.

You are not adversaries here; you are teammates striving for the common goal of peaceful coexistence. Maintain that attitude, and the disputes should be solved to the satisfaction of both parties.

PARENTING

Given that marriage is difficult and a couple's biological children can cause stress that leads to straying, then a second marriage with stepchildren can cause innumerable and often insurmountable problems. It is often a case of an adult caught in the middle, being pulled between two sides, and having to make a choice—the new spouse or the old children.

Previous theories about marriage must be modified or abandoned, leading to better understanding and control of a new situation. Particularly when children are involved, the marriage must evolve slowly as those involved cope with their new environment and try to maintain a balance in order to survive.

Because two parents may handle the same situation very differently, it's critical to analyze each person's background and become aware of the parenting styles in the families of origin. Unfortunately, not all men and women ask questions during courtship in order to shed light on such issues as the level of parental involvement, values, discipline, educational goals, and amount of time spent with the children.

The traditional roles that parents and children assumed in the "good old days" do not apply successfully to the dual-income families of the nineties. It's been said that the family is the woman's domain, and that's where she asserts herself. Men, on the other hand, may deal with the family from a much more removed level. A lot of dissatisfaction exists among women who believe they're doing it all. It's critical for couples to discuss their position in the family and how they should react in given situations.

Tradition is a significant emotional component of family life. When two partners bring to a new marriage contrasting perceptions about role models, behavior, and even what to serve at holiday dinners, they may be forced to re-evaluate customs that are dear to them. It may be necessary to adjust to, and compromise with, your partner, perhaps to establish new family policies altogether that reflect the needs and wants of the new family.

Inasmuch as we are human beings with limitations, this is not always easy. We are required to adapt to new ways of thinking to make the relationship work. Even though "communication" is a hackneyed term, the need for constant and open interaction can't be stressed too much or too often. If one partner withdraws, failure is almost a certainty.

Dave, a very prosperous doctor, hired a financial advisor to handle his personal investments and set up a pension plan for his practice. Not content with providing financial advice, the advisor started to give him advice on how to live his life and improve his self-esteem. Dr. Dave started to attend seminars, which took him away from home. His wife, Marie, had her own religious convictions and didn't feel the need to go along. The travel turned out to be a way for him to meet other women, and have affairs along the way. After a year and a half Marie found out that he had been carrying on with another woman. When this woman came to town, Marie hired a private investigator, who followed Dave and the woman to a hotel, where he was able somehow to get a camera in the room, and videotaped them making love. Marie's first comment on viewing the tape was, "She's so fat!"

The next day Marie followed her husband and the woman to their sailboat and confronted them. At first she was devastated. She is now in divorce proceedings.

She had known something was up because he'd been acting strangely. He had, in fact, asked her to go to a couple of seminars; she went once but didn't care for the experience.

Marie and Dave were married for fourteen years. It was the second marriage for both. He had two children from a previous marriage, and she had three, but the family never really connected. After all those years they were still arguing about the kids. What had initially attracted Dave to Marie was her confidence. He had always said he wanted a strong woman. Now he found her to be opinionated and bossy. She tried to force him to talk, but the talk always ended in confrontation. He said she nagged him, and he had long ago concluded that the best way to get along was to pull away from her. The ideal compromise here would have been for both to agree to talk about the important things and spend less time on trivial matters, but in the last year of their marriage, Dave simply shut off, and Marie didn't know it. He had made the decision to leave without even telling her. He joined a self-help/motivational group, so instead of coming home and working on his relationship, he came home and chucked it.

MARIE, FORTY-FIVE, DIVORCED:

"I didn't consider it nagging. I thought I was constructively trying to help my husband to be a better person. He doesn't have the self-control. He really didn't want to work on what was wrong with him. He just wanted a quick fix."

☙ ☙ ☙

MARIE'S FRIEND SAYS:

"Marie is beautiful and did everything to perfection. She orches-
trated everything and could just put everything together. She was
an asset in Dave's business. She knew how to present her husband, the doctor, in our small town as a real pillar of society and
the community. She was a good PR person for him, but she was
also very opinionated. She would always call him on stuff—for
instance, if she didn't like what he was wearing. She color-coded
his clothes so that all those tagged orange went together, and the
green, and such. From socks and shoes to shirts, ties, jackets,
and pants. Everything was color-coded. When she first married
him, she threw all his clothes out and started all over again. I
think after fourteen years he couldn't take it anymore. He had to
reinvent himself. But he went out the back door instead of
talking to Marie and trying to work on it. To me he lost all his
integrity by doing it this way.

"It's been very difficult for Marie to accept the fact that not
only did he trade her out but he traded her for some bimbo. She
worked so hard to stay thin and look good, buy the perfect clothes,
have the perfect parties. It was a total rejection of everything she
was. The bottom line is, I think Marie is very opinionated, and I
don't think she allowed them to grow as a couple. She wanted to
be right all the time, and you can't always be right—you never are.
She talked all the time and insisted she was right. My husband
and I used to comment on that. There were things that caused
him to look someplace else, and I think she has to accept the
responsibility for that. It's a reality check. You have to look at yourself first and then start pointing because you're never going to
grow if you don't look inward. If you don't think about what you
did or what you didn't do together to make it work, you'll make the
same mistake again. This is her second marriage, not her first."

🌱 🌱 🌱

SECOND MARRIAGES

Merged Families

JOHN, FIFTY-SEVEN, HAPPILY DIVORCED:

"Would I consider remarrying? I'd rather go out for cocktails with Dr. Kevorkian!"

🌿 🌿 🌿

Remarriage has become an accepted—and even expected—ritual of American life. Fifty percent of all marriages today are remarriages for at least one person. Thousands of recycled couples with children under the age of eighteen tie the knot each day. By the year 2000 at least 50 percent of Americans will be involved in a stepfamily—the simplest situation. Even more complex are multiple-family systems in which the husband and wife have children from the current marriage and other offspring from, perhaps, two or three previous marriages.

With all of these youngsters living in the same household—with the frequent movement between all the different families that share custody—meeting the needs of the adults as well as the children can be very difficult, and especially challenging if the family members hold unrealistic expectations about a problem-free stepfamily. The interpersonal dynamics and inevitable frictions that exist when two people get together are likely to be intensified when the family unit becomes more complicated. For example, a strong man and a dependent woman may balance each other to a degree, but if a dependent child enters the picture—one who has a lot of needs—a conflict-ridden dilemma arises for the dependent female. As personality traits become exaggerated and loyalty conflicts arise, the family becomes dysfunctional. In many new unions women feel torn between their husband's and their children's needs. With a new marriage comes a change of regime and rules, which often leads to resentment.

Parents might not recognize the hazards when they are dating. However, after the relationship grows more concrete and a marriage takes place, youngsters are apt to change their behavior and their attitude toward Mom's or Dad's significant other.

Two people can fall in love and marry with no idea of how their children will be affected. In most cases the problems don't manifest themselves fully until a legal union takes place and the two families begin to merge. Competition between family units may occur, perhaps exacerbated by different economic or educational backgrounds. External forces and economic considerations lead to future issues and problems. It is essential for both partners in the marriage to develop a sophisticated understanding of what motivates stepchildren.

Here, again, a united front must prevail.

MARLENE, FIFTY-TWO, SAYS:

"When I met Joseph, his daughters were away in college, and he didn't see much of them. They seemed to like me and welcome me into their father's life. As soon as we got married, one daughter became very needy and seemed overly attached to her father. She exhibited behavior toward him that was inappropriate for a woman twenty years of age. I found it very scary and I didn't understand. My husband said I just didn't understand the father-daughter relationship. He will never admit his children do anything wrong."

☙ ☙ ☙

It is extremely important that the couple come together and keep a united front in these instances. Unfortunately, what often happens is that the parent of the child becomes defensive and feels pulled in half.

THE MEDIA FAMILY VERSUS REAL-LIFE DRAMA

It would be beneficial to many people in merged families if the media took responsibility for presenting stepfamilies realistically. Many children who grew up watching *The Brady Bunch* were shocked when their own stepfamily didn't run as smoothly, when the cute problems of the TV show were replaced with real-life emotional issues that are difficult to work out.

Much of the conflict in merged families arises from expectations we all have of what a family is supposed to be and how we're all supposed to feel about one another. People tend to hold tight to fantasy when conceptualizing life in their cozy new stepfamily. They harbor misperceptions and make incorrect assumptions about how life will be.

If you have been married before, you're committed to the success of your new relationship. You want to do it "right" this time. Perhaps you thought there weren't going to be issues, adjustments, compromises, or obstacles. But there are always issues in life. The fantasy has to crash.

For example, the expectation "Love me, love my children" is not realistic. We cannot expect a newcomer to the family to care the same way we do about our children when he does not feel the same level of emotional involvement. Nor can we realistically expect our new mate to elevate us immediately to a position higher than that occupied by his children. If the spouse has not been married before or doesn't have children, he may feel threatened by having to share time and affection with the spouse's children from a former marriage. It is essential to learn to work through the issues. A dilemma may appear fairly mild at first but can mushroom when not dealt with in a timely manner.

When a new household is created by remarriage, two interpersonal systems go into action: the newlyweds' relationship to each other, and their role as parents to the youngsters. The couple's bond is crucial because it forms the new leadership team. Interaction with the child is also extremely important, and in order to have a happy family, both systems must succeed. The goal is to achieve a balance.

Second marriages often fail because of the parenting process, not because the husband and wife aren't getting along. If being a parent is difficult, being a stepparent is harder still. You are more cautious and more worried about what you're doing with another person's child. You try your best to be accommodating even under the most stressful circumstances because you want this marriage to be better than your last one. Unfortunately, the only guarantee is that this marriage will be different. Although each merged family is unique, they are all plagued with a similar set of problems and complications inherent to the situation.

> *I don't believe man is woman's natural enemy. Perhaps his lawyer is.*
>
> ☞ SHANA ALEXANDER

SHARED CUSTODY

When custody for either one's own children or the stepchildren is shared, the potential for conflict can be enormous. First are the practical matters of making certain everyone is where they're supposed to be on the correct day and at the right time. The children need to adjust to differences in rules and routines and the stress of living in two homes with various sets of people. It takes time and patience to accept all the changes and set up new daily agendas. And too often children are used as weapons or as unwitting spies against the estranged spouse. The stepparent-in-residence is caregiving every day, dealing with car pools, mealtimes, stomachaches, homework, and financial matters, and deserves credit for his or her ever-expanding involvement. A long time may be needed before a deep and abiding love develops between stepchildren and stepparents. Sadly, some biological parents feel resentful and jealous of the situation and try to disrupt it, whether by verbal slurs or by pointing out that the stepparent is not the "real" parent.

Many men have told me that the transition was just too traumatic and too difficult, and that, finally, they didn't even want to come home. If problems aren't dealt with as they come up, they often intensify over time. To build a foundation for a healthy stepfamily, the parents and children must accept and respect, rather than scorn, the differences between them and their new housemates. Understanding makes it possible to act and react more kindly and humanely. Acceptance leads to a more peaceful and loving environment. By keeping the lines of communication open, stepfamilies will prevent problems before they get out of hand.

The process of surmounting the obstacles that occur in various stages strengthens a stepfamily. When the small successes begin to add up, the housemates are on their way to a successful new family life. Problem solving takes time and understanding; most people have to work very hard at it, but the rewards are great.

Shelah, happily married thirty-eight years, says:

"I break a successful marriage into three equal parts. The first part is being the right person, and the second part is picking the right person. You're looking for the right fit. The third part is having similar goals. If you're with a man who's been married before, I think it's important for you to state that you will have this relationship and make this commitment, but if you're going to break the commitment, then it's over. If you state it up front and he really believes you, it may be a deterrent. If one side or the other breaks the agreement, the whole relationship is changed."

❦   ❦   ❦

ADULT CHILDREN

Adult children have very strong opinions about what their parents should or should not do, and they tend to be very vocal in expressing their point of view. Family issues that were never resolved when the adult children were youngsters can explode years after the fact. Any unresolved family issues from when the children were young are going to emerge in the adult children, particularly if the parent remarries. A mature adult who has resolved his or her conflicts will not have a severe emotional reaction to the marriage of a parent.

Even though it's not their responsibility to do so, adult children may assume a caretaker role and tell their parents whether or not to remarry, how to handle their finances, where and how to live, and how to behave in general.

Adult children make very powerful demands on their parents that younger children wouldn't dream of making. Often adult children are selfish. They are concerned, for instance, about inheritance. How will the marriage of a parent affect them financially? Don't forget that everyone in business is motivated by the WIIFM theory: what's in it for me? And finances play a key role in second marriages.

CONFUSED ALLEGIANCES

The husband-wife-child triangle requires a great deal of pushing and pulling and juggling to work. Consistently choosing one family member over the other, regardless of the circumstances, is never fair to anyone.

When something causes a parent or child to react angrily, it's sometimes difficult to know how to remedy the situation. First, the true target of the anger must be discovered. Second, if young children are involved, the parent must try to maintain a reasonable attitude that promotes dispute resolution and problem solving.

The Ex-spouse

The extended family takes on a new meaning when the former spouse is a part of the clan. Entering a new marriage does not necessarily signal the end of the old one. Sometimes a concerted effort and conscious decision must be made to let go of the past and the feelings one still carries for a former mate. After a hostile divorce, and a remarriage to a new love, the husband and wife are united against a common enemy— "the ex." But residual anger toward an ex-spouse is excess baggage lugged along into the new marriage. A key factor in moving forward is resolving old issues. Newlyweds must tie up loose ends, resolve the grief of time lost, and let go of their anger. The goal is to leave the past, and old resentments, behind and embrace a positive lifestyle with your present family. When the ex remains friendly toward the family, a more delicate situation exists. Even if two people don't love each other anymore, they may still have affection and respect for each other. The new spouse should not try to undermine or feel resentful of that congeniality.

When a second wife resents the friendly communication between her spouse and his ex, her own insecurities are coming into play. Be careful here! You don't want to force your husband to *defend* his ex against your criticism. You might send him back to her understanding arms! A new couple must work together to feel safe and secure in their marriage and untroubled by the continuing interaction with the ex.

The Dearly Departed Ex

Many people assume that a second marriage is easier if the former spouse isn't living, but often that's not the case. Usually the widow or widower harbors no negative feelings about the dead. That person becomes a saint. The new spouse is thus left with an impossible task: comparing favorably to an angel, or competing with an urn on the mantelpiece. Reaching closure on previous relationships—good and bad—is essential to achieving a fuller and healthier transition into the new partnership.

Relatives can also be a problem. You and your spouse may be in love, but that doesn't mean everybody else automatically loves each other. There are solutions that will keep most people—even unfriendly new relatives—happy. Whom to invite to the important family events and who sits next to whom may seem trivial matters, but, actually, they are key concerns if hurt feelings are to be avoided. Some couples may choose to celebrate Thanksgiving and Easter separately, with their own families of origin, rather than offend his or her parents by going to the other in-law's home. If "You go your way and I'll go mine" works, then it's a very reasonable solution.

On the other hand, if you hold the typical American belief that families ought to be together on holidays, and you define "family" as your current spouse, a problem could result. Feelings of rejection may be very hard to deal with if a spouse doesn't choose to spend holidays with you. Your own expectations are key here, and if they clash with his, something's going to have to give. Either you'll have to change, he will, or the situation will, in order to avoid constant conflict.

There are no dysfunctional families, only dysfunctional people. Your goal is to help a group of relative strangers, with disparate histories, backgrounds, expectations, and beliefs, grow into a successful, healthy family. You want to make your husband happy so that he will stay; you want your marriage to endure. It's a process that takes time. By understanding the nuances and dynamics of the new situation, you will be able to accept rather than judge, enjoy rather than criticize.

You cannot shake hands with a clenched fist.

☞ INDIRA GANDHI

Professional Advice from a Behavioral Therapist on How to Deal with the Extended Family

Emily says:

"What happens a lot of times in stepfamilies is that here's you and your husband, and here's your family that you brought with you. The weight of these children is pulling you apart. It shouldn't happen, but it is. The advice I'm going to give you is to strengthen the tie. In any family therapy the most important thing that can happen is that Mom and Dad unite. There's two of you, in one partnership. Sometimes we talk about how diffi-cult it is to be a single parent, but one of the things you don't have to deal with as a single parent is someone else's influence over your kids. I don't believe that one way is better than the other; I just find that they're different. If you were a single parent, and now your kids are grown, you've had the experience of focusing only on your kids, with no one around to second-guess you. Now, when your kids are grown and his kids are grown, it's essential that you and your husband keep the lines of communication open. This means that if you don't like what happens with his kids, you've got to talk to him about it.

"You might think that you shouldn't have to deal with his kids, and with everything else you don't like, but you do. Everyone comes with a package. One of the choices you don't have is to change the package. The choices you have are about only you, and where you want to be. Building a relationship is like building a house together. That house holds your life, your hopes, your dreams, your past, all the baggage that you bring, everything about you. It also holds your partner's baggage, his past, what he hopes for the future, what he's struggling with today, everything about who he is. And together you build this beautiful, intricate, complex structure that holds all of these things. The sturdier the house—the more solid its foundation—the better your relationship. Because if that house is sturdy, it will remain standing through the worst of times. So both partners should really focus on building the house, on nurturing and nourishing your relationship so it's strong enough to deal with all of the pull and the push and the onslaught of issues, including the problems that adult children can bring.

One way to communicate is to focus on your own feelings. If you start a sentence with 'Your daughter did . . . ,' the subject of that sentence is his daughter. Or 'You aren't dealing with your kids . . . ,' the subject of that sentence is your spouse. Make the subject of the sentence 'I.' You can make the same point but say instead, 'I feel scared when . . .' 'I feel uncomfortable when I see your son . . .' Train yourself to make an 'I' statement. 'I feel so angry . . .'

"It might be helpful to talk about the fact that difficulty in your partnership may mean learning to give up some control. You've gone from being in total control of your life to sharing your life with someone else. You may wish to articulate your own inner confusion and misgivings: 'I see things happening, and I don't know what I should say or what I want to say. I don't know what feelings I have that are legitimate, as opposed to what I just feel threatened by.' When you put the focus on 'I,' then you're opening up to him, you're making an invitation, and he's more likely to respond sympathetically: 'Oh, I don't want you to feel that way,' or 'That's not what it means.' If he chooses to air his side, then listen to him. Respond warmly: 'What was that like for you? Tell me about it.'

"Think of a time when your kids were little, and they hung all over you when you were trying to cook dinner or make a phone call, yelling, 'Mommy, Mommy!' You only half listened, and they, in turn, became more persistent. You probably learned that if you sat down with your kids and gave them your undivided attention— 'How was your day at school?'—they'd get done telling you in about five minutes, run off, and do something else. This situation translates well into the situation with your partner. If you're too busy defending yourselves to each other, beneath your words will always lie the real, unheard, message: 'There's not enough love for me here, you don't love me enough, you're putting me second . . . I have to fight to get you to listen . . . what about me . . . what about me . . . what about me . . . ?'

"Another concept that can be helpful is the idea of detaching with love. This is a way of trying to deal with a situation without your heart and soul getting trampled on in the process. It's a hard concept to learn, but it can be particularly helpful when dealing with the extended family of your beloved. If his family doesn't accept you with open arms, stop expecting them to. Instead, try to maintain some distance and objectivity by simply observing their behavior. You will probably find that you can usually anticipate what will happen, and when it does, you can enjoy your own private joke. This is a kind of empowerment, and an excellent way to maintain a sense of humor through it all. Being able to say to yourself, 'Well, I saw that coming' is very reassuring in itself.

"One way you *can* safely vent without incurring negative ramifications, is to write a 'letter'—to your partner, or to any one of his family or friends who may be causing conflict.

Here are the guidelines for the letter:

1. You do not have to be fair.
2. You do not have to be nice.

3. You do not have to be right.

4. You can be as rude, as crude, as blaming, as unkind, as you want to be.

There is a good reason for writing this 'letter.' You can tap and vent and externalize all the resentment and anger that you have built up. Because even though you may have already exploded and expressed some of it, there's a whole lot more inside that he's never heard. (You never send the letter.)

"Someone did a study once on depressed people. The study involved three groups of volunteers:

1. The members of the first group received no treatment for their depression.

2. The members of the second group saw a therapist regularly.

3. The members of the third group kept a journal.

"The first group showed little or no improvement over a specific time period. But groups two and three—the people in therapy, therapist visitors, and the journal writers—showed clear improvement over the same time period, at very similar rates. Basically, then, a journal does the same thing as a shrink. The magic doesn't lie in anything a therapist says; a therapist merely provides the environment for you to come in and explore the issues that you're dealing with. The letter technique I've just described has the same benefit as keeping a journal. It allows you to examine all the pieces of the puzzle, to turn them over and ask, 'What are they?'

"So writing a letter—one that's never meant to be posted—is bound to be therapeutic. Just remember: don't sensor it, and don't judge it, if you want it to be truly effective. And, above all, *don't tell your spouse about it!* Destroy it!"

🌿 🌿 🌿

CHAPTER TEN

Sensuality, Seduction, and Sex . . . The Good Stuff

RICHIE:

"My wife knows how to put the happy in 'Mr. Happy.' Most women have to make that a priority!"

🌿 🌿 🌿

RECLAIM THE SENSUAL SELF. Here's the fun part: making your relationship wonderful and romantic. Think of it as a return to splendor, and fall in love all over again. Experience passion on a different level. You're going to rekindle the desire by changing your behavior and letting the pleasure of your sensual femaleness awaken. You will relearn how to be happily married by doing more of what works and less of what doesn't. You will create a combination of visual excitement, emotional intimacy, and sexual intensity that will lead to lifelong sexual pleasure.

If you can't afford to hire the string quartet to serenade him on your anniversary, and skywriting is out of the question, there are other alternatives. But you've got to make an effort to work on it. Money is not the issue here; being well groomed and well dressed can mean dressing only in blue jeans and a white blouse and sneakers. Create your own image . . . be an individual.

In these hectic days of dual careers, you will have to make time, even if it's just to go to a movie and hold hands. With children around, you'll have to make an even greater effort. Surprise him with a romantic act like sending him flowers at work. And if the way to his heart is through the kitchen, familiarize yourself with it. Take a cooking class.

SEX

You're busy, he's busy; you don't have time. It's not always easy with children, or an aging parent, living in the same house. If you don't plan for sex, it's not going to happen, so make a committed effort. If you are exhausted and too tired from work to get into the mood, not much is going to occur to anyone's satisfaction. Simple affection and touching are necessities of keeping intimacy alive in a relationship. Cards or notes left in the bathroom or stuck in his pocket remind him of you. You need to put aside quality time for emotional closeness and the bedroom. Many happily married men told me they arranged sex dates with their spouse. For instance, if you know you can sleep in on Saturday mornings, set aside weekly time for "Sexy Saturday" every week, and let nothing interfere with that time for special playfulness. If you find yourself alone for a few hours in the afternoon, take a nap together. You need to figure out ways to stay connected to your partner. If you are geographically separated, use the fax, mail, phone, or florist to communicate. Don't be afraid to be racy and suggestive in your message, and never underestimate the value of phone sex. It's the next-best thing to being there. It can ease his loneliness and eliminate the need to search for excitement elsewhere. Be sure he can't get you out of his mind even if your job or his creates a physical separation. If you really want the relationship, you're going to have to work at it. Remember, if you don't use it, you lose it, and your loss is somebody else's gain.

Surprise him with a spontaneous gesture of sexuality like checking into a motel and greeting him wearing erotic lingerie. Recreate the newness and playfulness that were there during the initial attraction. Pay attention to each other, and don't take each other for granted. Stay in tune with what the other enjoys sexually. Make it happen; be an active participant.

> *"The best way to hold a man is in your arms."*
>
> ☞ MAE WEST

RICHARD, THIRTY-THREE, SAYS:

"A close married friend of mine never wore a wedding ring, but he's learned to wear one now to attract a certain kind of woman—the kind who *doesn't* want a commitment. He's run into a lot of problems over the years when a woman falls in love with him and wants a commitment. He had a really bad situation when a woman went to his wife, and his marriage has gone downhill ever since. Now, he wants the ring on in order to keep away women who want a commitment. It's the screening thing."

🌿 🌿 🌿

Love and Lust

Men love sex. They think about it more than women, they want to participate in it often. They enjoy a woman who loves sex and who sometimes takes the initiative to make it a little different. The woman who "submits" only occasionally and can't wait for it to be over is not going to be the big winner here.

Many women don't want to be bothered with sex. If you have lost your desire for sex, this is *your* problem alone, and I recommend you seek help from a qualified therapist. It is not reasonable to expect your husband to stay faithful to you with no outlet for his sexual needs. If you enjoy sex but find his needs don't match your own, you will probably benefit greatly from couples therapy.

Bed sex is great, but you might want to think about being a little adventurous. Many men told me their advice to women is to keep it exciting. Here's the perfect opportunity to be a little risqué. Make it an unforgettable erotic encounter in a new location—on the ground under the stars, in the bathroom at a boring dinner party, on the floor in his office or up against the copy machine—the more off-beat it is, the more intense and the more turned on he will be. The element of danger is an intense aphrodisiac. The fear of getting caught produces that rush of adrenaline that brings its own excite-ment, which heightens the sexual experience. Oral sex in the back-seat of a limo can be exhilarating, especially with the driver unaware. Men love oral sex and good sex, and if they get it at home, most will stay home. If they don't, they will go elsewhere.

The good news is that you don't have to be twenty-five with the perfect body. You just have to love and nurture your man with care and consideration. Get a copy of *The Sensuous Woman*, by J. It's essential reading and tells you how to perform oral sex competently. Invest in sexy lingerie, something silk or satin, and short. A bustier can be alluring; cleavage always captures attention. Make a concen-trated effort to avoid floor-length nightgowns or cotton tees and socks on a steady basis. With just a few surprising changes, your man will soon be inclined to seek sexual satisfaction in the only sensible manner: with you.

MEN LOVE:

- Playful, uninhibited recreational sex (Try licking whipped cream or chocolate syrup off each other's genitals.)
- Confidence
- A woman who loves her sexuality
- Sexual variety (the shower, the hall closet, the kitchen floor)
- New positions (your being on top)
- Noisy sex
- Oral sex
- Foreplay
- Sexy lingerie (How do you think your husband would like to see you in bed?)
- Candlelight and oil massages

MEN DON'T LOVE:

- Kids or pets allowed to walk in and out of your bedroom unannounced
- Staring at the ceiling during sex
- Serious sex
- White cotton panties with the days of the week written on them (What happened to your lingerie?)

ADVICE FROM HAPPILY MARRIED WOMEN

- Tell him you love him every day.
- Shower together often.
- Don't take a fight to bed.

- Work at being sexy.
- Greet him at the door.
- Make him feel important.
- Don't criticize.

Plan quiet dinners à deux. Cook him his favorite meal and turn the phones off. Appeal to his senses and seduce him with delicious aromas, candlelight, and you.

SEXY FOODS

- His favorite dinner (even if it's meatloaf!)
- Champagne
- Good chocolates
- Grapes (you can peel them for him)
- Strawberries or any fruit you can dip into whipped cream or melted chocolate
- Fondue
- Caviar
- Cold chicken, fried chicken, or anything you can eat with your hands (except french fries)
- Olives
- Cannoli (or anything else you can suck the middle out of)
- Artichokes
- Oysters
- Chinese food (you can eat it in bed)
- Soufflés

FOODS THAT ARE NOT SEXY

- Carbonated water
- Pigs in blankets
- Fast foods
- Onions, garlic, or any other pungent spice
- Anything that gets stuck in your teeth
- Corn dogs
- Fried dough
- Aerosol cheese
- Tofu
- Sweetbreads
- Tripe
- Veal (it could turn into a political issue)
- Beans
- Mayonnaise

"I live by a man's code, designed to fit a man's world, yet at the same time I never forget that a woman's first job is to choose the right shade of lipstick."

☞ CAROLE LOMBARD

WARREN, FIFTY-ONE, SECOND MARRIAGE TO FORMER
SECRETARY, SAYS:

"I don't think there's anything we haven't reviewed, I don't care what it is. We don't have an ambiguous relationship. I don't think marriage is a great sport, but it's not a science. All couples have their same battles. They all want to be loved; they all want to be touched; they all want love and affection. You can't survive without it. The only point of being a couple is to be loved and touched—otherwise, why bother? Forget whether it's a wife or subordinate or a peer or somebody above you. I wanted somebody there was a link of communication with. The thing that seems to make my present relationship work is that we're on the same wavelength. I've never had that before with anybody. We're chugging along with the same goals in mind. Who knows if that can happen forever? Whether it's a consulting relationship or a marriage relationship, we agree that this is what we're going to do. That's the way I run my business. It's the key to success in any relationship. Anne and I have this situation where we get laid and we do business together. That's real hard to do, and it's very unusual. If we manage to pull this off, we'll probably be one of the few couples who have actually been able to earn money together, have a relationship, have a great sex life, and keep the whole thing going on. We never planned it this way, it just worked out this way. We love each other, we're mad about each other. I'm happiest when I'm sexually satisfied. Life is a raft; you're on the raft, or you're off the raft. I want to be on the raft forever. One day at a time doesn't work. You have to have a plan. If you're a couple, it's got to be more global than that."

🌾 🌾 🌾

Men require a good deal of attention. When you were trying to extract a lifetime commitment, he became your focal point. Your thoughts concerned your future together. But somehow, his role in your life has diminished and the poor guy ranks behind kids, your job, laundry, and sheer exhaustion. What does it take to prioritize and treat him in a way that reminds him of those glorious precommitment days? Not that much, and the rewards will be great.

THE MAN WHO WOULD BE KING

Some time ago I was picking up my husband at the airport. I'd come home a couple of days before him from a trip. I had talked with him that morning and could tell he was tired and in need of a home-cooked meal after so much restaurant dining. I stocked the refrigerator and prepared his favorite dinner. I took two chilled beers in a cooler to the airport, as he often wants a beer when he gets off the plane. I was waiting at the gate to greet him when he got off with one of our married male friends. The man was annoyed and embarrassed that his wife was not there to greet him. "She's always late," he said. "I've been away for weeks, and there's probably no food in the house either." And then he said something sort of jokingly, but in reality we all knew it was true.

"I'm the king! And I want to be treated like a king when I come home. She doesn't work, I make all the money, and she can't even pick me up at the airport!"

He was verbalizing what most men probably feel. He wanted attention, and instead she didn't think it was necessary. Without knowing all the dynamics of their marriage, I couldn't help agreeing with him.

The average man is more interested in a woman who is interested in him than he is in a woman with beautiful legs.

☞ MARLENE DIETRICH

TERRIFIC TIPS FROM MEN WHO STAY

- Give him his space.
- Respect him in public.
- Celebrate ordinary moments.
- Treat your man like a king now and then.
- End every telephone conversation with "I love you!"
- Keep communication open and make time for each other.
- Remain a wife when you become a mother.
- Learn to ignite passion.
- Give little tokens of affection for no reason.
- Make the relationship work.
- Communicate, communicate, communicate.
- Don't overspend.
- Go on a sunset picnic.
- Make your partner "the most important person to know."
- Stay lovers for the rest of your lives.
- Keep it exciting.
- Show signs of affection.

THE TEN-STEP FORMULA FOR
A SUCCESSFUL MARRIAGE

Step One

Be an available, willing, and adventurous lover.

Step Two

Show your husband how much you care. Stroke his ego and compliment him. Cook him his favorite dinners. Become a good listener and stay interested in him and what goes on in his life.

Step Three

Make an effort to be an exciting person yourself rather than totally predictable. Plan special events and mystery trips to keep life exciting. Send the kids and the dog to your parents' or a friend's for the weekend.

Step Four

Don't become overly dependent. Maintain your own goals and interests.

Step Five

Give him space and trust. Don't demand an accounting of every minute of his day or every dollar he spends. Give him the freedom to pursue his interests and friendships.

Step Six

Remain his best friend and most ardent supporter. Tell him and show him how much you love him.

Step Seven

Spend time together. Share in leisure activities and interests. This is a great opportunity to get to know each other on a different level, keep the relationship exciting, and have something new to share and talk about that isn't a mundane household issue.

Step Eight

Surprise him with flowers or a gift for no apparent reason. Never let him forget you when he's out of your sight. Put a photo of yourself in his briefcase. When he's packing for a business trip, carefully place a pair of perfumed sexy panties in his suit pocket.

Step Nine

Perform your share of the household chores without making a big deal of it. If you don't like the setup, renegotiate at a preset monthly meeting rather than constantly complain.

Step Ten

Hold monthly business meetings to discuss goals, money, and unexpected financial emergencies.

JACK, FIREFIGHTER, MARRIED TWENTY YEARS:

"I stay because I love her and she is my best friend!"

🌿 🌿 🌿

A Stayer in His Own Words

Steven, fifty-seven, says:

"Although we did not actually meet until 1974, Anne Marie and I grew up in the same part of our town and attended the same grammar and high schools. In fact, her father and his three brothers were alumni of the college my sibs and I attended. We were also fraternity brothers who had met through fraternity events.

"Our meeting in 1974 came when Anne Marie was appointed to the local library board I was serving on. Anne Marie's first husband was a child diabetic. He died of a heart attack in 1976 while playing golf. Since we saw eye to eye on the important issues of the day, after a respectable period of time we began to date. This caused a few tongues to wag at the old library. The rest, as they say, is history. We were married in 1981. My brother's wedding toast: 'I have always said it would be a cold day in hell when John got married.' On that particular January 3 the Eagles beat Minnesota in a play-off game, and the temperature was seven degrees. We honeymooned in, of all places, Sarasota, Florida, where it was a balmy thirty degrees.

"The simple answer to your question 'Why do men stray?' is I don't have the slightest idea. I am a stayer. To try to explain why, I have searched the remaining gray cells and have fallen upon three thoughts that while just as inane as many of my others, seem the most germane to our topic. They are: family upbringing, having a wonderful wife, and, as Tiny Yokum from the long-gone comic strip *L'il Abner* once opined, 'No man is an Ireland.'

"My father always said if he ever strayed, you could have seen it in his face the minute he walked in the door. Divorce and playing around weren't dinner table topics. My father had too many good stories to tell from politics and from his work, first as a prosecutor and then as a judge. As for us kids, we didn't know anybody from a divorced family. Besides, we were too busy with school, sports, and raising hell. We were also born too early to have been taught by TV talk shows, Hollywood, and the like that cheating is permissible and you don't have to stick it out if things get a little rough.

"The shock of my life came when I was fourteen. Our next-door neighbors got divorced. To top it off, they had been separated for years and no one had told me. He was always coming and going, whether cutting the grass, playing touch football with us, or just gabbing. Our neighbors had stayed married until their son graduated from college.

"Ours was a suburban middle-class neighborhood of the forties, fifties, and early sixties. The men went to work, the women stayed home, the children were chased off to Sunday school, and the family stayed together. Thoughts of 'extracurricular' activities were not just not condoned, they weren't even thought of.

"I know many guys and a few women who either stray regularly and/or are divorced. Of my childhood friends, also products of the same middle-class values, only two are divorced, and no one admits to straying. The two were divorced because their spouses strayed. One, whom our crowd hadn't seen for years until a high-school reunion, was so embarrassed he couldn't even tell his old friends. But enough about upbringing. You get the picture. I must be dull. Nobody told us about straying. Staying was the thing to do. I guess it helped to be raised in a great environment. Nobody was around to tell us we were victims of society, so anything goes. But it was fun growing up.

"Likewise, it's fun being with my mate. We speak the same language. Similar backgrounds help. Anne Marie is charming, intelligent, warm, and caring. She laughs at my jokes . . . sometimes. She is also discerning and a problem solver. She has my love and respect, so why would or should I stray? Furthermore, as empty-nesters with the financial means, we have too many good adventures to look forward to. So I'm staying, and that's that.

"Finally, I was forty-two when we married. I would not trade marriage for those single years if I could. Real companionship is wonderful. Being a bachelor ain't what it's cracked up to be. Tiny Yokum, the poets, sages, and songwriters, all got it right— 'Man needs his woman and woman needs her man.' Enough said."

❦ ❦ ❦

And some stay, albeit unhappily. This is a strayer waiting to happen.

SEAN, AGE FORTY-EIGHT, COLLEGE PROFESSOR, SAYS:

"I don't know what to say about staying and straying. It sounds like something a herd would do. I guess my experience has been that women have an overwhelming need just to have a man. Having one of her own is really what's important. One day you realize she doesn't give a shit about you and your needs, as long as she 'has' you. So why bother? It turns out there wasn't anything really 'mutual' going on—she had just gotten what she wanted. Okay, so then I feel justified doing my own thing, after postponing it for fifteen years. I was totally exhausted and my wife had no idea. And she really never cared to know. Oh, great. So that makes me an idiot too.

"That's one element. Another thing that happens is a woman drying on the stem. Because she never listened to you and what you wanted, and made her own dreams of what she was going to get out of your life together. And since this didn't turn out, she dries up and makes your life horrible. Your every happiness becomes a source of irritation to her, since she has decided not to separate and not to be happy. But in any confrontation, you're faced with how much she loves you and needs you and adores you . . . tears, and gnashing of teeth and . . .

"Another is that a woman studies you and knows when you eat and do just about everything else but doesn't really care to go from this vegetative interaction to other sorts of interaction. And the woman who lies and conceals and . . . finally, you don't know what she does. She tells you what she calculates you want to hear. Forgets she ever said it if you find out it's a lie. Tells you she loves reading, carries a book at all times when she's trying to get you, and then never reads another book in twenty years because 'there's no time.' Someone who promises but never delivers on the promise.

"If I stay, it's essentially because I feel someone raked me over, on the one hand, and I feel so devastated I don't know what to do. Another reason I stay is because every time I talk about leaving to my children, I have to endure a crying session, which I can't bear. Another reason is that I had a plan of how to make things work out, and in a day-by-day, more perfunctory, way I continue to put the plan into effect. What for? I don't really know.

"And I have strayed . . . to work, where I can carve out a space for myself. And I make the effort to communicate with my children in an ever more personal way, and I wait.

"And I hate myself for waiting and find that I never know when the moment when I can or should leave may arise. And I keep thinking of my youngest child, who in three years will finish high school. Is she the reason I don't stray? Did something break in me? Is that the reason? Is there anything out there worth it? Is that the reason? Isn't to stray to become *the* stray, to be herded in again? Do I want to be herded in again? No, I think I'll do my own thing. But how much of doing my own thing has to do with straying and staying?

"So in this chaos I currently live in, there is a great stability to staying. You certainly know what you're not going to get. You have a certain pattern, and you have a certain command of certain spaces, and you avoid something of the tears. I don't stray, for the most part, in the way you may be thinking. In fact, in many ways I'm straying by staying. Straying into the exploration of myself and what I'm interested in and what I like. That doesn't imply much of a satisfying sexual life; that I miss—but here I surprise myself again. I really thought it was very important and certainly thought I couldn't do without it. And here I am—mind over matter just like they used to preach, and I never knew what the hell they were talking about."

❦ ❦ ❦

MARRIAGE MAINTENANCE 101: HOW TO KEEP HIM COMMITTED FOREVER

- Put your relationship before everything else (even yourself).
- Keep the "dance of romance" alive.
- Keep a sense of humor and don't take life too seriously.
- Keep a strong faith in each other.

- Give him overt signs of affection; squeeze his hand under the table at a dinner party; better yet, run your hand up the inside of his pant leg.
- Write him a poem or a song.
- Create enchanting romantic evenings right down to the music.
- Take breaks from each other once in a while.
- Sleep together and touch.
- Make a point to do things together.
- Renew your vows.

MARRIAGE BENEFITS

You might want to point out to your spouse that it might be wise for him to stop walking on the wild side. According to a recent *Dateline NBC* "Healthwatch" story, "Keeping the knot tied can help you live longer." Men appear to benefit a bit more from marriage than women. One study suggests that married men earn more and experience an increase in sexual satisfaction.

Marriage—there are a lot of reasons to take the plunge: love, happiness, security, but that's only part of the picture. Marriage can help you live longer. Consistently, studies have shown that people who are married have better health and survive for longer periods of time than people who are not married, whether they're separated, divorced, or widowed.

There's something about social support that makes people psychologically healthier, that makes them feel better, and that in turn causes a whole series of biological pathways or patterns directly related to good health.

Some studies suggest that people with healthy relationships tend to have stronger immune systems, lower blood pressure, and reduced stress hormones. Personal relationships seem to give us the strength, the resilience, to be able to operate in the most effective way.

Even though marriage has its share of stress, those stresses often force you to pay attention to the things you might ignore on your own, like your health. You're more likely to buckle up, or to be carted off to the doctor if you have a cold or some other illness that hangs on longer than it should. Being with someone can help you live longer. It's important for people to maintain intimate contact. Marriage almost always leads to a longer, healthier life.

> *The purpose of life, after all, is to live it, to taste experience to the utmost, to reach out eagerly and without fear for newer and richer experience.*
>
> ☞ ELEANOR ROOSEVELT

In the final analysis we must look at ourselves and ask why women are so disloyal to other women. What is a woman doing having a sexual relationship with a man who is married to someone else? She is causing the other woman grief, and most likely she is ultimately causing herself unhappiness.

There are many phases we go through in a marriage. As we change and grow, and the emphasis shifts away from securing the commitment to securing our own personal satisfaction, problems often occur. It is essential to keep the team communicating through these stages of change and growth.

The pursuit of one's own goals and happiness is a big responsibility, and it is a choice available to us all. If the marriage fails, you can still go on, and apply the lessons you've learned in future relationships. The main thing to remember is that you are in charge. There are always two ways of looking at every situation: "I couldn't get there because of my circumstances," or "I got there in spite of my circumstances." You decide!

Index

W

wardrobe, strayer's, 62

women

    aggressiveness of, 84-86

    availability of "other," 50-57,
        77-81

    examples of "other," 86-94

workplace, women in, 79-80

About the Author

SUSAN KELLEY, a former professional model and television writer, is also the author of *Why Men Commit* and *Real Women Send Flowers*.